# QUESTIONS AND ANSWERS

## FUNDAMENTALS OF THE ESOTERIC SCIENCES

By
**MANLY P. HALL**

THE PHILOSOPHICAL RESEARCH SOCIETY, INC.
Los Angeles, California

ISBN NO. 0-89314-801-6

L.C. 79-6527


*Copyright © 1965*

*By The Philosophical Research Society, Inc.*


First Paperback Printing, 1979

Originally issued under the title
*Questions and Answers, Fundamentals of the Occult Sciences.*

Library of Congress Cataloging in Publication Data

**Hall, Manly Palmer,** 1901-
Questions and answers.

1. Occult sciences.   I. Title.


BF1411.H353   1979          133'.076          79-6527
ISBN 0-89314-801-6

*Published by*

THE PHILOSOPHICAL RESEARCH SOCIETY, INC.

3910 Los Feliz Boulevard, Los Angeles, CA 90027

Printed in the U.S.A.

# TABLE OF CONTENTS

## RELIGION
### PART THREE

## LIFE AND DEATH
### PART FOUR

# THE MYSTERY SCHOOLS
## PART FIVE

# HUMAN REGENERATION
### PART SIX

# HEALTH AND THE LAWS OF PHYSICAL LIFE
### PART SEVEN

## SOCIAL AND POLITICAL PROBLEMS
### PART EIGHT

## MISCELLANEOUS
### PART NINE

# PREFACE

LL men suffer from certain reasonable doubts concerning Life and Truth. These uncertainties arise from the complexities of social existence and the contradictions everywhere present in the institutions of Theology and Science. It is the purpose of the Ancient Wisdom teachings to answer these reasonable doubts with reasonable answers. A philosophy that cannot explain the mysteries of life intelligently and practically is not worthy of attention.

Wise and enlightened sages and scholars have lived in every period of the world's history. The opinions of the deeply learned are useful to all men. Each human being must evolve his own philosophy of life, and all personal philosophies should be based upon adequate and enduring foundations. At no time is man left without an ever-present guide in time of trouble. The great philosophic literature of the world contains answers to all men's questions, but these answers are frequently hidden in a ponderous literature which average persons lack the temerity to attack. It is therefore useful that the teachings of the wise concerning the practical problems of life should be rendered available in a convenient and digested form.

In the course of many years of lecturing and teaching, a great number of questions have come to me for solution and explanation. I have classified these questions into general

11

groups for greater convenience in answering. In the present work, the questions have been so worded as to cover as many angles as possible of the subject treated. The answers are derived from the philosophies and religions of many nations and ages. The teachings of most of the world's great spiritual and intellectual leaders are incorporated into the commentary material.

For the sake of clarity and simplicity, I have not in every case gone into elaborate details concerning references and authorities. Usually, the source of the material is obvious. Details are unnecessary, for the answers represent recognized systems of thought widely studied and generally accepted.

If this book of *Questions and Answers* proves to be a practical aid in the understanding of certain metaphysical and spiritual problems, I shall publish further volumes taking up other problems and other aspects of the subject.

# FUNDAMENTALS

## PART ONE

*QUESTION—Where do we come from? Why are we here? Where are we going?*

*Answer*—Twenty-five hundred years ago Gautama Buddha wandered up and down the roads of India asking the learned saints and philosophers three questions: Where? Whence? Whither? Many wise and mysterious truths Buddha learned from the holy men, but not the answers to these three vital questions. After years of wandering, disillusioned and discouraged by human ignorance of fundamentals, Buddha found within himself the answers which the world could not give. These answers are the essence of Buddhism, and, spreading from India, they have come at last to be part of the general heritage of the race. The philosopher acknowledges that Buddha solved the riddle of life.

The solution may be summarized as follows: Life is eternal, and man's appearance upon this earth for three score years and ten is but an episode in an existence made up of innumerable episodes. The Orientalist thinks of lives as beads strung together upon a thread of endless consciousness. Life is an endless unfoldment toward the Real. It is consciousness growing up through experience, with its beginnings in the immeasurable past, and its ultimates in the immeasurable future.

To the question: Where did we come from? the philosopher answers—up from unimaginable beginnings in immeas-

urable eons of time. Up through an inconceivable diversity
of forms, through types and species entirely forgotten, from
worlds that have long since finished in space, up through
electrons, atoms and cells, up through grains of sand, through
plants and animals; up through all the races that have gone
before. All the past is man, for never was the time he was
not, and he shall cease to be never. We were the Atlanteans
and Lemurians, we were the Neanderthal man and the Cro-
Magnon who scratched their dreams of life in rude pictures
upon the walls of caves and painted in strange forms their
exploits and their dreams. We were Egypt, Greece and Rome.
Our roots are in the Infinite, and we are growing up
through the finite to finally, in the end, emerge once more
into the Infinite. Our age is not measured in millions or
hundreds of millions of years, but in vast eons. All we have
accomplished is stored up in ourselves. We are always becoming, for we are part of the immortal elements of existence.
We are the progeny of Unknowable Space.

Why are we here? What we call here and now is but
the present moment of infinity. We have always been somewhere, and we will always be somewhere, and an instant of
this *somewhere* we call *now*. We flow from the past into
the present, and, never ceasing, flow through the present into
the future. Our present state is the substance of the past,
built upon it. We must forever do the next thing next. We
are here to learn, to experience, to improve, to progress.
We are living down the past and up to the future. We are
what we are now because of what we have been. Our present living is but an episode of a greater existence. The true
reasons for our living are not evident here, and this little
life is truly "rounded with a sleep." Law brings us into life,
law is the purpose of our living. Each is in the place he has
earned for himself by past action, and each is earning for

himself a better place in the ages which are tomorrow. Hundreds of times we have been born into this world, and hundreds of times more we shall be born again, and all our births and deaths together make up one greater life, the purpose of which is but dimly perceptible to our present imperfect realization. We bring into this life the strength and weakness which are the products of our previous living. In this life we refine a little more the fabric of ourselves. Having learned a few more lessons, having found a little more truth, having done a little more of good, having come a little closer to perfection, we call this life finished, depart for a little time, and then return to continue the task of searching for the Real.

Where are we going? As we are the past, so we will be the future. Through all the evolution of races and empires we pass, contributing our part to each generation and each age. Thousands of lives stretch before us in the human evolutionary cycle. We are still struggling with our humanity, striving to perfect ourselves in the human virtues, groping for wisdom and courage and the beautiful, trying to bring into moderation all the extremes of our irrational impulses, yearning after the One, the Beautiful and the Good. We are indeed on a journey that is endless. For no matter how much of truth we find, the ultimate of truth lies beyond. No matter how much of wisdom we achieve, infinite wisdom lies beyond. In the end, like some great processional, we move in majestic file across the sky from star to star, past all the suns in their glory, to vanish at last triumphantly into the Infinite from whence we came—ever striving, ever yearning, ever gazing into Space. The progeny of the Infinite, we seek to be mingled again with our Eternal Source. In this search time is an illusion. An instant is as a thousand eons, and a thousand eons are as an instant. It is not time but accomplishment that measures all things. Our final rest is beyond the stars; not in a static heaven of theology's misconception, but as an Eastern poet has said: "We come at last back to the root of the dream, one with the Eternal."


QUESTION—*What is God?*

*Answer*—The answer to this question is largely a matter of viewpoint. Creation is God personalized. God is creation impersonalized. If you mean by a personal God an old man with whiskers seated on a golden throne, then such a concept is irreconcilable with philosophy because, to philosophers, such a concept of Deity is purely idolatrous. An idol can exist in the mind just as surely as it can in wood or stone. Idolatry is the personification of universal principles. The impersonal God of the wise is the Sovereign Good, inconceivable and immeasurable, which abides in everything, enlivens and supports all things, ensouls existence, and in the terms of Brahman metaphysics, extends to the very circumference of Space. Justice is impersonal, truth is impersonal, law is impersonal, virtue is impersonal. All the great and noble events that lift man to the heights of universal achievement are impersonal. Universal survival depends upon the impersonality of that vast Cause which supports the entire scheme of life. Yet the impersonal God is not distant; in fact, is far more intimate than a personal divinity could possibly be. The God of philosophy is not anywhere, but everywhere. At a certain stage of human growth, man achieves to the realization of the insufficiency and inconsistency of a personal God. The mind then demands an impersonal Agent at the foundation of action. It is not the purpose of philosophy to reconcile the concepts of a personal

and an impersonal God; only growth, development, and unfoldment within the individual can result in that state of mind
in which the personal divinity fades away, and consciousness
discovers that vast and all-sufficient Spirit which abides in
the star and the grain of sand.

*QUESTION—What is creation?*

*Answer*—Creation as a process is a term employed to signify the process of objectification or the flow of invisible forces
into visible manifestation. Creation is not technically the beginning of anything. It is merely ever-existing forces assuming temporary patterns. These patterns remain for a certain
time and then dissolve again. The term for this dissolution
is either disintegration or decay, but neither disintegration nor
decay really signifies the end of anything. It is merely the
breaking up of a pattern, the elements of which are in themselves immortal.

Theologically speaking, creation is the formation of the
tangible universe under the direction of cosmic or universal
intelligences, called the gods. Actually, creation is the incarnation of the gods or supreme principles that build around
themselves the form of the world, even as the incarnating
human spirit builds its body. Therefore, the worlds are the
bodies of the gods subject to growth, maturity and decay, even
as the human body is subject to the vicissitudes of change.

One definition for creation is "release into tangibility."
Thus the creative power of man is the power to engender
forms or patterns through which ideals, forces, or concepts
are given expression or material release. When more profoundly considered, however, creation is the building of shells

by which great forces are limited or circumscribed or intensified into prescribed areas. Creation is described in some of
the ancient Oriental books as the "curdling of space." Out
of ever-existing elements, impermanent forms are fabricated.
These forms, whether they be electrons or suns, are temporary
manifestations of eternal forces. These forces exist whether
they manifest or not. Creation is the process of their manifestation, and disintegration is their process of retiring from
manifestation.

The word *creation* may also signify that which has been
created or manifested. In this sense, it is a term to describe
the infinite diversity of manifestation in which man lives,
moves, and has his being, and of which even the visible parts
of man himself are examples. Creation is an inconceivable
extension of forms, each of which is the embodiment of the
forces. Forces all manifest according to law. Therefore
creation is geometrical or mathematical, and is completely
patterned. The order of creation is proverbial, but creation
itself is merely a symbol, the visible shadow of things unseen.

Creation is the body of Sovereign Intelligence, and
man's effort to understand the Real is closely linked with
his contemplation of forms and laws. The Real is invisible
in itself, but is manifested in every atom of creation. The
world is the Real made form. Man is the Real made soul.
The urge that created the world is the same urge which, in
the human soul, inspires man to create beauty, to invent,
to devise, and to express his inward convictions by means of
symbolic forms. Creation is the inward conviction of reality
manifested through its most appropriate symbol. Plato calls
creation the divine animal, the first of living things, from
which all lesser natures are suspended.

*QUESTION—Explain the great time cycles.*

*Answer*—The ancient Brahmans, meditating upon the mystery of creation, perceived with the inward eye the great cycles of time that make up the ages of the world. The Greek philosophers and the Egyptian priests also calculated the duration of ages and the various divisions of time that constituted cycles or periods of manifestation. In most ancient systems, the calculations were directed toward the discovery of the length of the Cosmic Life, or, in the Oriental terminology, the Age of Brahma. The unit of measurement was the human pulse beat. These were grouped together to form minutes; the minutes were grouped to form hours; the hours were compounded into days; the days were massed into years; and the years were arranged in great patterns called Yugas and Kalpas.

In the Hindu system, there is a unit cycle called a Yuga. Four Yugas constitute a Maha-Yuga or Great Age. A Maha-Yuga equals 4,320,000 human years. Seventy-one Maha-Yugas equal the period of the reign of one Manu, or celestial king of the world, the total being 306,720,000 years. There are fourteen Manus ruling in a Day of manifestation, and their total reign equals 4,294,080,000 human years. The Sandhis, or connective twilights, which bind the reigns of the Manus together are equal to six Maha-Yugas or 25,920,000 years. These added to the previous figure complete the reign of fourteen Manus as 1000 Maha-Yugas, or 4,320,000,000 years. This total is called a Day of Brahma. The Night of Brahma, or the Pralaya, contains the same amount of time, so that one Day and Night requires 8,640,000,000 years. A year of Brahma consists of 360 such Days and Nights, or 3,110,400,000,000 human years. One hundred such Years of Brahma constitute the Life of Brahma: 311,040,000,000,000 years.

To the Hindus, Brahma is the Supreme Being of the manifested universe, and the so-called Life of Brahma represents the period of Brahma's incarnation. At the end of his life, Brahma retires into a subjective existence to remain for an inconceivable period of time before re-manifesting in a new Life or Age.

Humanity, at the present time, has just passed the 5000-year mark in a Kali-Yuga, or Dark Age, equivalent to the Iron Age in the Greek calculation. The length of a Kali-Yuga is 432,000 years, but within this collective time are smaller cycles of ascent and descent. But the age of obscuration, as it is called in the Hindu classification, has yet 427,000 years before its completion. At the end of the Kali-Yuga, or Dark Age, the world will pass into the Krita-Yuga, or Golden Age of the gods, which will then continue for 1,728,000 human years.

A summary of the opinions of the Hindus on the matter of the Yugas, particularly the Kali-Yuga in which we now live, will set forth the significance of these time calculations in their relationship to human experience.

In the sixth section of the *Vishnu Purana*, Maitreya asks Wisdom, personified as Parasara, concerning the method of the dissolution of the universe, and how men might know that a greater or lesser Kalpa is coming to an end. The sage, in answering him, gives us a viewpoint on life which we cannot fail to heed with the present stress that surrounds us in the world. The wise man, answering Maitreya, says in part that there are Four Ages: Krita, Treta, Dvapara and Kali, and that all life is made up of these Ages, repeated again and again. These periods may be called, for simple understanding, Birth, Growth, Maturity, and Decay.

Quoting from the great sage Parasara: "In the first, Krita, is the Age which is created by Brahma" (birth of things).

"In the last, which is the Kali Age, a dissolution of the universe takes place." (Kali is the principle of blackness, disintegration, death, and decay.)

Maitreya then says: "Oh, venerable sir, it behooves thee to give a description of the nature of the Kali Age in which the four-footed virtue suffers total extinction."

The ancients taught that the destruction of virtue was the end of all things, and that the universal dwelling place collapsed, consumed by the flames of immortality. During the Kali Age, environments destroy themselves and destruction avenges itself. That which is false falls a prey to its own falseness. Thieves steal from each other until crime, destroying itself, gives birth to a new virtue. Peoples vanish, races are overrun, and those who think they are proud collapse.

Speaking in the terms of the Puranas, but leaving out the more obscure paragraphs, let us consider how Parasara informs his student that the coming of the end is to be foretold when Kali, the goddess of destruction, shall rule the planet. Parasara states that the end will be heralded by a number of things, in the midst of which Kali will devour creation and a newer and purer world will take the place of that which has gone before. Literally thousands of years ago the following indications of the beginning of the end were given to the Brahmans, and, through the Puranas, to the world. Below are listed numerically those statements which have any bearing upon either our lives or our customs as they are extracted from the words of Parasara:

In the Kali Age:

1. Marriage will be celebrated according to the rituals. But the spiritual rites of the communion of lives will be lost.

2. The student of wisdom shall be without a Master, for the powers that connect the spiritual protector and his disciple will not be in force.

3. The laws that regulate the conduct of husband and wife will be neglected.

4. All celestials and spirits and lights, and all orders of life, will be considered as one and equal.

5. Fasting, austerity and liberality, practiced according to the pleasure of those by whom they are observed, shall constitute piety.

6. Every trifling property will make men proud of their wealth.

7. Wives will desert their husbands when they lose their wealth, and the rich will be considered lords.

8. He who distributes immense wealth will be considered as a master of men.

9. Accumulation of wealth will be spent in ostentatious dwellings.

10. The minds of men will be wholly occupied with earning money and that will be spent on the gratification of selfish desires.

11. Women will follow their own inclinations and be given up to pleasure-seeking.

12. Men will endeavor to acquire riches even dishonestly.

13. No man will part with the smallest fraction of his wealth at the sacrifice of his own interest.

14. All people will consider themselves as equal with the Brahmans. (God-anointed or illuminated.)

15. Cows will be held in reverence only because they supply milk. (Meaning that things are only of value for what one can get out of them.)

16. People will always be in fear of dearth and scarcity, and will watch accordingly the appearance of the sky.

17. Deprived of wealth, people will be perpetually subject to famines and other afflictions. They will never enjoy pleasure or happiness.

18. Children will pay no attention to the commands of their parents.

19. People will be selfish, abject and slovenly; they will be indecent, immoral in their conduct, and will ever attach themselves to the dissolute.

20. Householders will neither sacrifice nor practice becoming liberality.

21. Princes will plunder their subjects instead of protecting them, and under the pretexts of levying customs will rob the merchants of their property.

22. Everyone possessing cars, elephants, and horses will be a Rajah. (Meaning that possessions will be the measure of worth.)

23. Everyone who is feeble will be a slave.

24. Farmers will abandon agriculture and commerce and seek to gain a livelihood by the exercise of mechanical arts.

25. The poor, seeking sustenance by assuming outward marks of virtue, will become the impure followers of impious and heretical doctrines.

26. Oppressed by famines and taxation, men will desert their native countries and repair to those lands which are fit for a coarser grain.

27. The path of the Vedas (scriptures) being obliterated, the people having deviated into heresy, iniquity will flourish, and the duration of life will therefore decrease.

28. On account of the horrible penances enjoined by (false) scriptures, and of the vices of the rulers, children will die in

their infancy. Men will grow old at the age of twelve, and no one will live more than twenty years.

29. The race will possess little sense, vigor or virtue, therefore will die in a short time. The wise then estimate the approach of Kali when the numbers of the false increase, and the numbers of the virtuous decrease. For the respect to the teacher declines, and regard is cherished for the disseminators of heresy.

30. The principal caste will be the ignorant; the wise will vanish from among them.

31. Men shall say, "Who was my father? who was my mother?"

32. Gifted with little sense, the race will be subject to all sorts of infirmities of mind, speech and body, and will daily commit sin, and everything that is likely to afflict beings, vicious, impure and wretched, will be generated in the Kali-Yuga (black age.)

*QUESTION—What is consciousness, intelligence, and force?*

*Answer*—Pythagoras symbolized Deity as an equilateral triangle, a simple diagram presenting three equal faces. Simon Magus, the Gnostic, also made use of the triangle to represent the aspects of what he called the Profundity. The Cabalists represented the Godhead by the first three manifestations or spheres of the Sephirothic Tree. The Brahmans used the Trimurti or three-headed Brahma to represent causal energy. It will be found by an examination of various religious systems that the Godhead is almost invariably depicted as a trinity in unity. God is Life; Life in the spiritual world is called consciousness; Life in the mental world is called intelligence; and Life in the material world is called force. The divine quality, in its three manifestations, permeates and sustains the three worlds, called by Pythagoras the supreme sphere, the superior sphere, and the inferior sphere.

*Consciousness* is the condition of Self-knowing in which realization is intrinsic. Consciousness is therefore universal Self-knowing, the sufficient realization of the Self in all things. Only the gods are conscious, for only the divine beings are free from the limitations of the intellect and are azonic, that is, unlimited by the boundaries of vehicles as we know them. All beings have bodies, but only the more subtle and universal bodies are capable of sustaining the experience of consciousness. Man approaches consciousness in the mystical experience of illumination, but is not equipped by his present organism to sustain this state consistently.

*Intelligence* is individualized consciousness. By intelligence is to be understood the equilibrating and rationalizing faculty which is present in entities capable of interpreting consciousness only through an intellectual organism. Intelligence is consciousness limited to the consideration of imminent things in the phenomenal or exterior life. With intelligence we can understand living, but intelligence cannot understand Life. Intelligence is limited to the sphere of manifestations, and functioning upon abstract principles of form is incapable of understanding such principles as are formless, or without manifestation through form. Intellect is called by Plato the self-moving principle, because it is the apex of all action, contributing purpose and decision to both nature and man. The philosopher knows, however, that he must rise above intellect if he is to find the Real.

*Force.* When consciousness is interpreted in terms of energy or vitality it is called force. Motion is evidence of life, even as intelligence is evidence of life. Force is circumscribed by the laws of the Cosmos. All energies flow according to certain restrictions, and act according to certain geometric patterns which Plato called archetypes. Everywhere in nature, we see force creating patterns, or revealing the law and consciousness, along lines of crystallization or energy-extension. Man's thoughts could not be interpreted into actions without the aid of the physical energy principle or consciousness as force. The motion of suns, the growing of plants, the arts, trades and crafts of mankind are all expressions of physical energy. But each of these expressions fulfills a superphysical purpose. Force by itself is purposeless and chaotic unless it is directed by intellect. Therefore, the Eastern philosopher says: "Force is the horse, and thought the rider."

In occult philosophy, it is taught that the universe is created by consciousness, sustained by intellect, and finally disintegrated by force. Therefore consciousness, intelligence, and force are referred to as Creator, Preserver, and Destroyer. By destroyer is meant rather the disintegrator—that which breaks up old patterns, but in no way adversely affects the life and intelligence within these patterns.

QUESTION—*What is spirit and what is matter?*

*Answer*—Spirit and matter are relative terms devised to signify two phenomenal conditions of one indivisible essence. Spirit and matter are the two fundamental aspects of Life. Spirit and matter are interdependent terms. One has no significance without the other, for matter is the least degree of spirit, and spirit is the highest degree of matter. In the sphere of mortals, spirit and matter are represented by good and evil, also interdependent terms.

By Spirit the metaphysical philosopher understands the active principle of life. This principle Plato calls the "unmoved Mover of all things." By this definition, matter becomes the passive principle; or, in the Platonic philosophy, "that which is moved" or receives unto itself the energy of the active principle. Matter, receiving upon itself what Boehme, the German theosophist, called the seal or signature of the spirit, is arranged into patterns or forms which we call bodies. A body or form is *ensouled matter,* or matter ensouled by spirit.

In the Cabala, it was taught that the Creating Principle appeared as a vortex of spiritual energy in the midst of space. This vortex the Jewish mystics called Kether, or the Crown of Life. From the Crown, rays of vibrant power flashed forth, impregnating all space. Space was regarded as atomic, or made up of infinitely small particles, each seed-like or, as the Platonists would have called them, "germinal." Universal Life, flashing into each of the germs of space, activated the life principle in these germs. As a result of this activation, the germs unfolded from within, outwardly. The term *spiritual nature* was applied to the life element in each of the germs, and the term *material form* was applied to the outer coverings of the germ. The evolving monad, as Leibnitz would have called these atoms, was growing up in space, and the dark mysterious essence in which the atoms clothed themselves was termed matter. Matter is entirely invisible in its ultimate state. What *we* call matter is form, a compound of spiritual energies and activated matter.

The Chinese signify this mystery by saying that the universe consists of three parts—heaven, earth and man. By heaven they mean not the sky, but causal energy. By earth they mean not the element, but the universal receptive capacity which receives into itself the emanations of the Creative Power. By man they mean not humanity, but all forms, whether of suns, moons, stars or man, which have arisen from the compounding of the two basic principles.

Spirit is universal. It is one eternal life, called by the ancients a sea or ocean of ever-flowing good. Forms are innumerable vessels into which life flows. But though the containers be many, that which is contained is one and undivided. There are many forms, but only one spiritual essence. Thus matter results in the illusion of diversity. Christian theology in particular fell into this illusion. It speaks not of spirit, but of spirits, and by this very statement denies the real fact.

Mystics of all races have long known that there is only one spirit in the cosmos. There are not divine spirits, human spirits, and animal spirits, but one spirit flowing through divine, human, and animal forms. As water pouring into a vessel assumes the shape of its container, though in its own nature shapeless, so spirit, flowing into forms, assumes the shapes of these forms and appears to assume the similitudes of its bodies. But the Taoists of China know that as the springs flow into the streams and the streams flow into the rivers, and all the rivers flow into the great sea, so evolution is the imprisoned life in all things flowing through innumerable forms back to the sea of its own universality.

*QUESTION—What are the seven laws of life?*

*Answer*—In different schools, different names are given to the great laws that control the universe. But it is generally acknowledged that the number of these laws is seven, that their influence is without exception, and that neither

God nor man can in any way alter or modify their influence. Man, by changing himself, may change his relationship to these laws and come into better harmony with the divine purpose, but the laws themselves are immutable. The following is one arrangement or conception of the seven great laws of life:

1. *Evolution.* That all things are unfolding is the first law of life. Evolution, or more correctly ideation, is a gradual release from within of the divine potency behind form. The growth of bodies and the development of form bear witness to the emergence of inward spiritual forces. The grain of sand unfolds into man, and the man unfolds into a sun. Among the axioms of the ancient alchemists, there is one that says: "there is a sun in every grain of sand; all is in all; one is in all; and all is in one." Evolution is the constant coming outward of the within of things. It is not life growing from one state to another, but life gradually emerging and assuming new appearances at each degree of its emergence.

2. *Cause and Effect.* Next only to evolution in significance is the law of cause and effect; or in human relationships, karma or compensation. It is the law of cause and effect which decrees that every action in the universe must be followed by an appropriate reaction, and to this there is no exception of any kind, at any time, for any reason. In the words of Buddha, "Effect follows cause as the wheel of the cart follows the foot of the oxen." In human affairs, cause and effect, as karma, decrees that every individual is individually responsible for his own actions, and that every action will produce a reaction equivalent in every way to the integrity of the action. The student should always remember that karma is good as well as bad. The only reason most people see more of retribution than reward is because their own

code of action has been more selfish than intelligent. Do not wait for good karma—make it now.

3. *Polarity.* All things in nature are dominated by the law of polarity and the correlative fact that poles are constantly alternating. The law of polarity in the universe is manifested in the relationship between suns and their planets, and also throughout nature in the principle of male and female or sexual differentiation. It should be remembered that the spiritual principle in all things is androgynous, but that in manifestation, it is always polarized. By the law of alternation, for example, the human soul, coming into life, incarnates in either a male or female body. In the process of reincarnation the sex of the body alternates, being male in one life and female in another. Even the earth itself not only has poles, but by a third motion is slowly reversing its poles, so that the South Pole will at some time be the North Pole. The law of polarity is universal.

4. *Reincarnation.* This is the law of evolution applied to the experience of individualized living things. The law of reincarnation teaches that all the kingdoms of nature are waves of life moving through form, or rather moving through levels of forms. Man, learning the experiences of the physical world, lives here not once, but many times, his life being really measured by the whole span of human evolution. In the search for experience, the human spirit returns to the physical world many times, there to work out its karma and perfect itself in the consciousness of the life wave.

5. *Vibration.* This law is the basis of all the differentiation in the universe. Spirit is a rate of vibration; thought is a rate of vibration; the universe is a complex of vibratory rates. Vibration is the first manifestation of life, and is the nearest thing to God that man can conceive. By discipline and effort,

man can raise the vibration of the cells of his own body. This is called refinement. Thoughts are vibrations, and therefore are capable of influencing those to whom they are directed. Music is vibration; color is vibration. If man can completely understand vibration, he will be master of most of the secrets of the world.

6. *Harmony and Rhythm.* There is a difference between vibration and motion. Actually, it is only a difference of intensity, but in the phenomenal life of man, an important difference is application. The law of harmony and rhythm shows that all motions in the cosmos are dominated by a certain flowing order. The universe does everything beautifully. Man, living beautifully, comes into harmony with life and moves with the rhythm of the world. By cultivating harmony and rhythm in himself, man becomes conscious of the universal motion which the Taoists call "Tao," the ever-flowing Reality. The Dervish Jelal-ud-din sought to whirl his own body in harmony with the rhythm of the spheres. It was said that Pythagoras alone, of all men, could hear the music of the seven planets. All the universe sings, and every atom is dancing to the rhythm of the suns.

7. *Generation.* This law teaches that in the world of form, all things must increase by the law of generation. By this law, only wholeness or completeness can produce. The law of polarity has resulted in a division of forms, in order that in each sex, part of the creative power could be devoted to the building of intellect. The law of generation therefore decrees, everywhere in nature, that the reproduction of any kind of form, emotion, or thought must arise from the union of two polar opposites. This is evidenced in the human brain by the two hemispheres that must combine their forces before even a thought can be born.

First study these laws to the degree that you are familiar with their workings, then look about you in nature and life and perceive how inevitably these laws work out. Having convinced yourself of this fact, live in harmony with these laws yourself, realizing that peace and security result from living the law, and not from trying to break it, evade it, or escape its consequences.

*QUESTION—What are the seven continents or epochs?*

*Answer*—In the secret doctrines of Asia, it is taught that the earth passes through seven ages or major changes in its physical nature. These changes result in seven major continental distributions, or, in more simple terms, the map of the earth presents, in the course of the planet's duration, seven appearances. The earth's surface is always changing to some degree, and these constant changes build up seven major patterns or surface groupings of land and water.

These seven groupings called continents support the seven races. Each new major change in the consciousness of living things demands a new environment in which to perfect itself. Life is like a great play with seven acts, and nature is constantly changing the scenery so that each act may take place in an appropriate environment.

The gradual cooling of the earth, which occurred in the dawn of the world, brought into physical solidity first the polar caps. The axial rotation of the earth being the slowest at the poles, these cooled first, producing the twin continents Pan and Isuvia. The North Polar Continent is called the Imperishable Island by Eastern occultists. It was upon this polar cap, in the first ages of the world, that the gods descended, and here all life had its physical beginning.

As the cooling of the earth continued, the second major continental distribution took form. The Greeks called this the Hyperborean World, a term that means the "land that is north of the winds." The earth's surface was still covered with mists and, with the exception of the polar continent, was subject to constant volcanic change.

The third continental distribution was approximately equatorial. The earth's crust had completely hardened.

This third continental distribution is called Lemuria. To this land migrated the various waves of life that had their beginning at the polar cap. Parts of what are now Ceylon, the Australasian Archipelago, Australia, and the central parts of South America and Africa, are remnants of the Lemurian continental distribution. The greater part of the Lemurian world is now submerged, involving the area of the Indian Ocean and the Pacific Ocean bed.

The fourth continental distribution is called Atlantean. The name is derived from Plato's description as perpetuated in the *Critias*. The principal center of the Atlantean world was a great continent extending from Labrador and Greenland on the north, to Brazil and West Africa on the south. The rise of this continent required millions of years, and it was slowly destroyed over long periods of time. The cataclysms that brought about the final submergence of Atlantis began more than a million years ago, but the last part of Atlantis, the island of Poseidonis, sank about B. C. 10,000. The continental distributions overlapped each other to some degree, and a considerable part of the Lemurian distribution was modified to form the Atlantean pattern.

The fifth continental distribution, called the Aryan, is that with which modern man is familiar. A great part of the land area of Atlantis and Lemuria remains, built into the new world pattern. The civilizations on these continents have been broken up, although strong centers of Atlantean culture still flourish in China, and Africa is still populated by the descendants of the Lemurians.

The sixth and seventh continental distributions are yet to come. It is widely believed that the center of the sixth continent will rise in the Pacific and will incorporate a considerable part of what is now called the Western hemisphere. The seventh continental distribution will probably be Asiatic; that is, it will be a new arrangement taking place in that part of the earth now involving Japan, China, and Siberia.

It should be remembered that Atlantis, Lemuria and all the old land distributions were not single continents arising in one place, but were land distributions affecting the whole surface of the earth. The development of each continent involves a considerable part of the land area of the preceding continents. In each case, however, the great cultural systems flourished from centers that have come to be identified as the whole continent. The highest civilization of the Atlanteans, for example, arose on the part of Atlantis which has now disappeared under the Atlantic Ocean. For that reason, many people believe that the submerged continent was all of Atlantis. This is not true, for large parts of land in Africa, Asia, and America, and a considerable part of Europe, were above the water during the Atlantean epoch. Possibly this can best be expressed by what we call Western civilization. We think of Europe and America as ruling the world in this epoch, but this does not mean that the rest of the world does not exist. The present Aryan distribution involves land on all parts of the earth, and so did the preceding distributions, with the exception of the Polar and Hyperborean continents which were formed before the entire surface of the earth had cooled.

For a discussion of the races evolving on the various continents, see the next question.

*QUESTION—What are the races of man?*

*Answer*—The ancient doctrines teach that during the present life wave, seven races (or, more correctly, species and races) will be developed. The first races were the Will-Born, sometimes called the Sons of Yoga, for they precipitated their Chayas or shadows through intense meditation. These shadows—the prototypes of bodies—were not as dense as our present physical forms, but correspond in state to a dense mist. The shape of these Chayas was very different from that of our present physical bodies. They were roughly globular and semi-transparent, with more opaque or denser areas distributed through them. These areas later became vital centers. The most highly evolved of these sensitized fields, which occupied approximately the upper pole of the spherical body, was the third eye, which, as the forms crystallized, retired from objective manifestation until it completely closed, or ceased to function as an organ of spiritual perception, during the Lemurian period.

Though the Sons of Will or Yoga precipitated these shapes, they did not actually enter into them, but remained suspended over them connected by etheric threads through which magnetic forces were transmitted. A somewhat similar condition still exists in the case of the animal, for the monads of animal life are still partly outside of the physical bodies. When seen clairvoyantly, the animal presents somewhat the same appearance as occasionally occurs optically in the case of double vision—two images not quite together—whereas in man the registration of the two is perfect. Having established their shadows, the Sons of Will began to "spin a web," uniting the shadows to themselves or, if viewed physically, uniting themselves to the shadows.

Milleniums of time passed, during which the Sweat-Born and the Egg-Born appeared, being various stages in the development of the mechanism of generation. During this whole period, the creatures were androgynous. The first races did not propagate at all, the Chayas remaining until the Pralaya destroyed them all; nor was the element of growth present. Later the shadows multiplied by fission—that is, in the way that cells multiply at the present time, the main difference being that the parts did not increase in size. The bodies, continually decreasing in magnitude, were finally destroyed because they were incapable of growth, and were soon reduced to a state where they could not serve as vehicles for organized life. In later species, growth was added, and what is now commonly called the "pudding bag" men appeared. The sacklike form was apparently tied at the neck, at which point the pineal gland extended as an organ of both sense perception and the rudiments of motion. It gradually developed into a pseudopod, somewhat resembling the fingerlike protuberance of the clam. These bodies, while far more dense than those of the Will-Born, were still entirely too attenuated to leave fossil remains, and anthropology will never be able to establish their existence, save through analogy or by studying the recapitulations of previous cycles of existence which appear in the developing embryo.

Still later we have the gill-cleft man. The atmosphere of the earth had not yet cleared, and the entire sphere was surrounded by a thick wall of humid semiliquid vapors. It was not until the clearing of the earth's atmosphere in the Lemurian period that lungs began to appear. By the fifth sub-race of the Lemurian period, physical bodies had taken on approximately their present appearance, except that they were extremely low in organic quality. The flesh resembled wood pulp in the very early Lemurians and showed a coarseness resembling beef in the later subdivisions. Giantism had then appeared, for form always runs riot until mind, demanding the greater part of the vital forces for its functioning, pulls down body to the degree that intellectual functioning increases. There were also monstrosities upon the earth due to the interbreeding of human and animal strains. This occurred at the psychological moment when the unfolding human cycle was recapitulating its animal development. At no other time could they have been generated and live.

In the fifth sub-race of Lemuria, approximately nineteen million years ago, the actual division of the sexes took place. This involved a cataclysmic change in the psychological organism of the evolving type, the complications being revealed symbolically in the allegory of the Fall of Man.

It is necessary at this time to pause for a moment and call attention to a special point that might otherwise definitely confuse the issues involved. Up to the time when the gods (the egos) took upon themselves the daughters (the bodies) of men and entered into them, two complete evolutions were moving side by side. Man was evolving in the spiritual worlds—that is, upon the higher planes of the earth—at the same time that he was building bodies upon the lower. In fact, in some of the traditions it is described how races were divided among the continents before the races had developed any temporal bodies whatsoever. When the Vahans, or vehicles, had gradually emerged from chaos into an organized state, two orders of evolution—the one spiritual, and the other physical—were actually united. Previous to that time, the bodies had no consciousness other than that which man experiences during dreamless sleep.

The later sub-races of Lemuria spread through the Australasian Archipelago, increasing in number and power and developing the rudiments of several new sense perceptions. They even built cities, and developed languages by imitating the sounds of nature in her various moods.

The fourth, or Atlantean, root race resembled our own in nearly all its biological attributes. The Atlanteans were the first to engage in warfare with its resultant disturbance in the life cycles. The birth rate therefore rapidly increased, whereas previously the Lemurians, some of them living for centuries, did not require as many vehicles for incarnation. It was also the Atlanteans who first began to dabble in magic, even to the point of breeding monsters by thought power. These creatures were incapable of reproduction, however, and, like Frankenstein's monster, turned upon their own creators. All these practices disturbed the astral light, permeating it with noxious psychical forces bred by the Atlantean sorcerers, and this finally brought about the cataclysm that ultimately destroyed the Atlantean civilization.

The fourth sub-race of the Atlanteans marked the real turning point of human evolution. During this fourth sub-race, bodies reached their present degree of crystallization. From that time on, life began the process of reabsorbing into itself the forms it had been exuding. The process by which this is accomplished is called by the profane "refinement," being simply the breaking up of the form patterns which, by their density, create the condition of materiality.

The fifth root race, of which we are a part, is well on its way along the ascending path that leads to liberation from the consciousness of form. For as the wise fully realize, form is actually a condition of mind; in fact, it is part of the work of the Will-Born, who meditated matter into being so that they might organize it into form. By the end of the fifth root race, the physical body of man will be far more attenuated than it is now, and the sixth root race will bring with it "the blue men from whom nothing can be concealed." The blue signifies ether, which is still somewhat visible to the physical perceptions of man as the haze that hangs at the base of mountains, this haze being part of the etheric double of the earth. In India, the god Vishnu is shown with a blue face to signify the highly etherealized substances from which his bodies are formed.

During the blue race, form will still exist, but will resemble somewhat the matter composing the planet Jupiter, which, while a solid, would be incapable of supporting physical man upon its surface. He would fall through it as he falls through water. As the etheric body asserts itself more definitely, both the arterial and venous functions will decrease, while the nervous activity will be greatly stimulated.

The sixth root race (not to be confused with the sixth sub-race of our present fifth root race, which will be the progenitors of the new cycle) will develop two spinal columns, representing an equilibrium of the sympathetic and cerebro-spinal nervous systems. The skin will undergo a definite metamorphosis, and all the sense-perceptions will be highly sensitized. During this period, the androgynous man will reappear, and it is affirmed by several occultists of note that at this time the larynx will be the organ of generation. In other words, creation will be through the spoken word.

At last, with the coming of the seventh race, the two spinal columns will be reunited into one, and the general appearance of the whole body will undergo great change and modification. The attenuating processes will have been carried so far that all the grosser elements will have been reabsorbed through transmutation into the spiritual nature.

At such time, it is declared generation will cease. The first race (which never actually died, but lived on in all the races that came after it), the adepts of the seventh round, as Sons of Will and Yoga, will awaken from the meditation that precipitated them into generation, to find the whole of this thing we call life to have been but a figment of consciousness. Thus it is written that when the Kumaras, or the virgin souls, awake from the seven dreams, they will discover that they were never actually in evolution at all, but that what we term evolution was actually taking place within them—a mystery of Yoga.

*QUESTION—Explain the difference between body, mind, soul, and spirit.*

*Answer*—The term *body* should properly be applied to any one of the several vehicles of manifestation which the ego or Self emanates from its own being to serve as mediums of expression or function. The most generally recognized bodies, in the case of man, are the physical, vital, emotional, and mental. Bodies are not necessarily visible, nor are they always tangible, to any physical sense perception. To use Plato's simple definition: A body is any structure or form to which energy is communicated.

*Mind* is variously defined in different schools of metaphysics. It is most generally accepted as the coordinated sublimation of bodily impulses. In other words, it represents the sum of the numerous instincts and impulses, enlivened or quickened by a ray of rational energy from that which the ancients termed the Self or the spiritual Over-Being from which personality is suspended. Mind is the mediator between Spirit and body, referred to as the common ground.

The position which the mind occupies in man—half way between invisible cause and visible effect—has given rise to nearly all the Messianic religious doctrines of the world. In several schools of philosophy, the Messiah is enlightened mind, which finally lifts the personality to Truth through its own nature.

*Soul* is a very loosely used term. The indiscriminate misapplication of terms causes endless confusion among the schools of metaphysics. Soul is generally regarded as synonymous with spirit, but the ancients regarded soul as an intuitional body built up in man by the assimilation of experience. All men perform wise and unwise deeds. These actions give rise to experience, and experience justifies action. No matter how much a man may suffer, if this suffering results in experience, it is worth all that it costs. Soul is the spiritual gold arising from the transmutation of the baser instincts and emotions. In the ancient Mysteries, the soul is termed the "robe of glory." It is the spotless seamless garment of transmuted emotion, thought, and action, which each disciple of Truth must wear when he seeks admission to the Hidden House.

*Spirit* to the ancients meant life; not life in its physical aspect of vitality, but rather that Universal Life Principle which pervades, animates, and sustains existence. Specifically, the term is applied to the causal substance in man, the abstract life energy, the abiding Reality in the midst of ever-changing appearances. To the Eastern philosopher, spirit is never regarded as individualized. One man does not have one spirit and another man another spirit. Spirit is universal. All diversity ends in spirit, and spirit is never divided. Thus, men are an innumerable race of personalities divided in form, indivisible in spirit.

*QUESTION—What are the seven bodies of man?*

*Answer*—Man is a composite being consisting of seven superphysical principles manifesting through the body, which is referred to as the eighth part of the soul. The superphysical principles are the causes of all the phenomena of physical life. Man's thoughts come from his mental nature, and his mental nature is the manifestation of his mental body. Man's emotions come from his emotional nature, and his emotional nature is the manifestation of his emotional body. The physical body is therefore a victim of the thoughts, feelings, and desires communicated to it by what the Greeks called the seven parts of the soul.

In their septenary classification, the ancients did not generally include the physical body, which is merely the container and manifestor of the seven active principles. We place it here, that it may appear in its proper position in the concatenation of ascending qualities. In occult textbooks the superphysical bodies are generally set forth in the following order:

1. *The Etheric body.* This is the etheric counterpart of the physical body, and is the sustainer and vitalizer of the material form. It controls growth and the digestive and assimilative processes, and repairs the damages caused in the physical body by the wear and tear of living.

2. *The Emotional body.* This vehicle is divided into two parts, the lower being the seat of the appetites and sensations, and the higher, the seat of the esthetic and constructive emotions. The emotional body also controls the motion of the physical form and directs the sensory perceptions with their instinctive emotional reflexes.

3. *The Lower Mental body.* This is the animal-mind body of the Greek system of philosophy, and the mortal or illusional mind of the Vedantists. It is the body of objective

thought, and controls man's personal decisions and all his mental reactions based upon education and environment. The perceptions and the mental-emotional reflexes have their origin in the lower mental body.

4. *The Higher Mental body.* This is the divine mind of the ancients. This higher mentality is the root of philosophical realization, the sphere of creative thinking. It is this mind that is manifested in the genius, and is regarded in most systems of philosophy as more than human. This is the Heroic Intellect of Plato.

The cycle of reincarnation carries the entity no higher, between lives, than the higher mental body, which is the apex of personality. Although the term "bodies" is sometimes given to the three higher parts of man, the word "principles" is more expressive. Above the mental world, man's personality is merged into universal qualities.

5. *The Buddhic Principle.* The fifth body or principle of man is the vehicle of illumination. The adept, lifting his consciousness to this plane, or inward level of thinking, finds here an extension of his realization from *thinking* to *knowing.* The term Buddhic means "inwardly enlightened."

6. *The Atmic or Causal Principle.* This is the highest differentiated principle in man and is his consciousness in an undivided and unconditioned state. It is from the Causal Body that the personalities emanate. It is the root of the phenomena of his lives. It is the Ever-meditating Lord who sits serene above experience—the Father in Heaven.

7. *The One.* This is the Universal Source, the common denominator of all living things, the eternal earth of Space and Spirit, from which grow all the seeds of the world, of gods, and of men. It is the inconceivable and indescribable

Source, called by the Egyptians the Trice-deep Darkness, and by the Jews, Ain the Boundless. In the Seventh Principle, all things are One.

The ego, or individuality, is the higher mental nature. The individuality is personalized in the lower bodies, and universalized in the three parts higher than itself. It is most important to the realization of all students that they understand that their vehicles or bodies ascend from personal and individual existence through gradual stages of impersonalization until, at the summit, all life converges to and is absorbed in the One First Principle. The intellect cannot ascend to this realization. Therefore, philosophy teaches that man must rise above thought to the three higher principles which are terms of consciousness. Even consciousness has divisions within itself. Man is capable of reaching the Real because he has a ladder of bodies within himself upon which he ascends through the disciplines of philosophy or the slower processes of evolution. Thus he finally reaches the Universal Reality, which is the ultimate of progress in our present cosmic system.

### QUESTION—*What is Truth?*

*Answer*—Pilate's question has been asked a hundred million times by the heart of man groping for the Real. Truth is a small word, a symbol of the vastest Principle conceivable by human consciousness. Most of the mistakes of humanity have been committed in the name of Truth. After thousands of years of human speculation, no adequate or appropriate definition of Truth has ever been devised. We can speak about it, but what it is we may not say.

No man possesses Truth, but, more and more, wise men are possessed by it. It is the Over-Reality, the Absolute Fact that can find no pattern in the world of relative things. Everything is Truth, but nothing manifests it fully. All forms, all thoughts, all feelings, all actions, are fragments of Reality. But even when all these fragments are put together, Truth is not perfect, for included in it are inuumerable factors of which the human consciousness has not the slightest awareness. Only the Real knows the Real, only Truth knows Truth.

For man Truth is integrity. It is most highly manifested in man's instinctive realization of the nobility of life. It is the urge in all things to be perfect even though man does not know what perfection is. It is the root of the urge to accomplish. It is that something which makes all creatures dissatisfied in themselves because they feel sure of some far distant and infinite Sufficiency.

In searching for the highest manifestation of Truth in nature, man has found that equilibrium, normalcy, and that permanence which avoids all extremes, come the closest to a satisfying standard. In living, Truth is virtue; in thinking, Truth is wisdom; in feeling, Truth is beauty; in action, Truth is moderation. Yet all these commendable things together are not enough. Truth is, most of all, the ever-evidenced Sufficiency. It is absolute reason, absolute security, transcendent completeness. In everything that is, there is a certain evidence of adequate purpose. All things are themselves, and there is a gloriousness about this fact that brings to the thoughtful mind a faint shadow of Truth. Truth is, and all that is, is Truth. And in the transcendent fact of Truth's complete and inevitable existence, man finds the strength for his endeavor, the courage of his conviction, and an ever-present sense of all-pervading Reality.

*QUESTION—Will the finality of life ever be known?*

*Answer*—It is difficult for a person who is part of a forever growing universe to even think in terms of finality. Ultimates are dangerous thoughts. They are intellectual barriers to those realizations of infinity which are natural to the inner life of man. Man reaches finality by becoming finality, for all ultimates are God. Man is as far from ultimates as he is from absolute divinity. The philosophers conceive no static states beyond action. To the Buddhist, that Nirvana which is the end of finites, is merely the beginning of infinites. When men grow too wise to be men, they become ever-growing wisdom. Occasionally we meet metaphysicians who suffer from the delusion that they will speedily achieve to the end of all human seeking and will repose individually in the perfection of ultimate accomplishment. These poor souls have been deluded either by themselves or by others. In the words of the old teaching, "life is ever becoming, but it never becomes."

# PHILOSOPHY

## PART TWO

*QUESTION—Give a definition of philosophy.*

*Answer—*To appreciate the scope and value of philosophy and its superiority over every other branch of learning, it seems appropriate to consider briefly the opinions of learned men relative to the importance and dignity of this noblest of human institutions. The quotations that follow are for the most part verbatim, but in a few cases we have slightly condensed the original statements, in no way, however, adding to or altering the meaning.

Hume: "Be a philosopher; but amidst all your philosophy be still a man."

Learning should never separate a man from his world nor cause him to feel himself superior to others; rather, it should bring him closer to the heart of mankind and bestow upon his soul a realization of the dignity of all life and the identity of all creatures.

Cicero: "Philosophy, rightly defined, is nothing but the love of wisdom."

The soul, ultimately disappointed in human relationships, must turn from its attachments to outward forms, and bestow its affection upon those imperishable truths which alone can satisfy man's yearnings.

47

Southey: "Philosophy is of two kinds: that which relates to conduct, and that which relates to knowledge. The first teaches us to value all things
in their true worth, to be contented with little,
modest in prosperity, patient in trouble, equal
minded at all times. It teaches us our duty to
our neighbor and ourselves but it is he who pur-
sues both that is the true philosopher. The more
he knows, the more he is desirous of knowing;
and yet the further he advances in knowledge,
the better he understands how little he can attain, and the more deeply he feels that God alone
can satisfy the infinite desires of the immortal
soul. To understand this is the height and perfection of philosophy."

From this definition it becomes apparent that sacred and
secular knowledge are but two aspects of one divine institution. True philosophy is not satisfied to reason only upon
mortal concerns, but rises to loftier speculation, intent upon
discovering not only the law, but the Maker of the law.

Gifford: "Divine philosophy! by whose pure light,
We first distinguish, then pursue the right;
Thy power the breast from every error frees,
And weeds out all its vices by degrees."

It is most fitting that a definition of philosophy should
come to us in verse, for as science is the prose of existence,
so philosophy is the poetry of living. By the perception of
divine realities, we finally poetize the dissonant themes of
life.

Epictetus: "All philosophy lies in two words:
sustain and abstain."

The wise man sustains his reason by feeding upon a sufficient diet of thoughts. He abstains from that which will bring sickness to his mind by eliminating from his thinking and living all thoughts and actions that are unreasonable and destructive.

Coleridge: "In wonder all philosophy began; in wonder
it ends; and admiration fills up the interspace.
But the first is the wonder of ignorance, the last,
the parent of adoration."

Only the philosopher possesses the power of intelligent appreciation. To the wise man, the wisdom of the universe becomes apparent. From the intelligent contemplation of existence, arises a full realization of the perfection of that Parent Cause upon which all creation hangs.

Cicero: "To study philosophy is nothing but to prepare oneself to die."

We may face the small issues of the day with ignorance and still preserve some small illusion of security, but in the presence of that great transition which is the inevitable fate of all men, our only security lies in some adequate appreciation of the Universe and Its Plan.

Quarles: "Make philosophy thy journey."

How wise was that old emblem-writer when he perceived that life is a journey in wisdom, action an experience in knowledge, and truth is the whole purpose of our being.

Epictetus: "The first business of philosophy is, to part from self-conceit."

A man who overestimates himself will underestimate his world. To be humble is to admit the greatness of the universe. Out of a becoming humility arises the capacity for understanding.

> Max Mueller: "Philosophy is the knowledge of the
> limits of our knowledge."

Beyond the small circle of the known, stretches an eternity of uncertainties. Of this the wise man is aware, but he has found security in the realization that beyond the eternities of the unknown again is the all-sufficient circumference of Truth.

> Aristotle: "Philosophy is the science which considers
> Truth."

Though Pilate's question remains unanswered, it is the opinion of the wise man that it is not unanswerable. The philosopher knows that there is but one way to discover Truth and that is to become Truth. Philosophy is the science of becoming.

> Bulwer-Lytton: "Real philosophy seeks rather to solve
> than to deny."

When the temple of wisdom is completed, much of its foundation will be made up of stones which sophists have rejected. There is no virtue in denying things as they are, but there is great virtue in discovering the reason for things as they are.

> Seneca: "It is the bounty of nature that we live, but
> of philosophy that we live well; which is in truth,
> a greater benefit than life itself."

To live without thinking, is to descend to the state of the brute; but to crown life with intelligent action, is to rise to the estate of the superman.

Lavater: "True philosophy is that which makes us, to ourselves and to all about us, better."

There is no merit in wisdom, there is no reward in knowledge, there is no comfort in faith, unless these things manifest outwardly, subduing the violence of action, and bringing us to a harmless mode of existence.

Nesbit: "The modern skeptical philosophy consists in believing everything but the truth, and exactly in proportion to the want of evidence; in making windows that shut out the light and passages that lead to nothing."

Philosophy is nothing if not noble; it is of no value unless it inclines the race to gentle virtue and noble action. To the measure that it fails to adore the One, serve the Beautiful, and venerate the Good, it fails to be philosophy.

Voltaire: "The discovery of what is true, and the practice of that which is good, are the two most important objects of philosophy."

Thinking is not merely an exercising of the mind, it is a directing of the mind. Only such as have organized thought to the accomplishment of some actual good are worthy to be denominated wise.

Shaftesbury: "The sum of philosophy is to learn what is just in society, and beautiful in nature, and the order of the world."

Philosophy is founded upon vision and experience—vision to perceive a noble end, and experience to modulate man's natural impulse to over-hasten the reformation of his world.

Plutarch: "Philosophy is the art of living."

The arts are sciences of the Beautiful, and if philosophy be the art of living, it must be the art of living beautifully.

Shaftesbury: "It is not a head merely, but a heart and
resolution, which complete the real philosopher."

Wisdom arises not from intellect alone but from the whole
life. It is built upon wise thinking, generous feeling, and
trained perceptions.

Thoreau: "To be a philosopher is not merely to have
subtle thoughts; but to so love wisdom as to live
according to its dictates."

Philosophy is first living, then thinking. The philosophic
life is the only foundation upon which a code of intelligent
action can be built.

Seneca: "Philosophy is the art and law of life."

By this Seneca implies that philosophy is a rule of procedure, a code by the living of which man becomes worthy of
happiness.

John Selden: "Philosophy is nothing but discretion."

By *discretion* we should understand that regulation of action
by which all intemperances are controlled, whether they be
of the mind or of the body. He who is discreet is above an
unreasonable act and may be justly termed wise.

Cowley: "To be a husbandman, is but a retreat from
the city; to be a philosopher, from the world;
or rather a retreat from the world as it is man's
into the world as it is God's."

The world of God and the world of man are not separated
by any distance other than the interval of understanding. As
we grow wise, we depart not into some distant country, but
rather we perceive the wise man's world emerging from the
very ignorant world of our own sphere.

Burke: "Philosophy is queen of the arts and the daughter
of heaven."

The wisest of the sages have always maintained that wisdom
had its beginning not among men, but among the gods, from
whom it descended for the salvation of humanity.

Seneca: "Philosophy is the health of the mind."

It is normal for man that he should think well, but the
blight of materialism has destroyed his birthright to wisdom.
It is therefore necessary, in this benighted age, for each man
to struggle valiantly if he is to achieve to a normal and
reasonable state.

Londos: "A true philosopher is beyond the reach of
fortune."

To be truly wise it is necessary to so love wisdom that
there is no place left in the mind for anxieties concerning the
temporal state. He who lives in desire for plenty or in fear
of loss, has no right to call himself a philosopher.

Sims: "Philosophy is reason with the eyes of the soul."

The intellect in itself can perceive nothing beyond that
which is intellectual, but the intellect, when quickened with
spiritual perception, bestows the philosophic viewpoint.

Hare: "The business of philosophy is to circumnavigate
human nature."

A philosopher must be fortified against himself. Philosophy
is a conspiracy against the inadequacy of ourselves. By it we
are given courage to act more nobly than is natural to the
human animal.

Lamartine: "Philosophy is the rational expression of
genius."

We may define genius as special aptitude, but when special aptitude is directed to the most important of all efforts, the perfection of self, it is termed philosophy. A philosopher is a genius who has discovered the most perfect use of his abilities.

> Joubert: "Whence? whither? why? how?—These questions cover all philosophy."

Whence—First Cause. Whither—to First Cause. Why—law. How—wisdom. From the Infinite to the Infinite we must proceed. The why of life is known only to the Maker; but from philosophy we learn how to fit ourselves into the plan of life and to prepare ourselves for final identity with our Cause.

> Carlyle: "The philosopher is he to whom the highest
> has descended and the lowest has mounted up;
> who is the equal and kindly brother to all."

Between heaven and earth stands the wise man. His earthy part has been raised to its highest perfection as the instrument of a divine purpose. The higher part, the soul itself, has become tolerant of the limitations of the body and, wise in its own weakness, is tolerant of the limitations of all other things.

In conclusion, let us define philosophy:

> The perfect science, and the science of perfection.

*QUESTION—What are the greatest systems of philosophy?*

*Answer*—Schools of philosophy are generally considered under two headings: Eastern and Western. The principal difference between the two schools lies in the concept of First Cause or God. Oriental philosophers regard Deity as a state or condition of realization, while Western philosophers regard it as a conscious or intellectual Principle. The ends to be achieved by the two schools are likewise irreconcilable. Western philosophy postulates the ultimate perfection of mankind in the production of a superior or divine type. Eastern philosophy postulates the ultimate absorption of man into the modes of consciousness constituting the Reality which supports the universe.

The principal schools of Western philosophy are the Platonic and Aristotelian, named for their founders. Plato excels in the profundity and scope of his thought, and Aristotle in the thoroughness of his examination and in the faculty of classification. The Christian philosophers of the Ante-Nicene and Post-Nicene schools drew the substance of their doctrines from Plato and Aristotle, and therefore cannot be regarded as the founders of independent systems. Probably the most important modern philosophers in the West were Francis Bacon and Immanuel Kant.

The Eastern schools include Brahmanism, Buddhism, Vedantic and Yogic philosophy in India, and Confucianism and Taoism in China. Unquestionably, Buddhism is Asia's great philosophy, and no school of Indian thought has escaped its influence. Buddhism, spreading into China, contributed its part also to the development of Taoism and Confucianism.

There have been many great philosophers both in the East and West, but if from among them all we must choose the greatest, Buddha and Plato stand pre-eminent. The intellects of these men are unsurpassed and unequalled in the records of human thinking. Both were mystics and occultists in the highest sense of these words. Both gave to the world great civilizing systems of culture and, for over twenty centuries, have been the constant inspiration of the noblest thinkers of the human race.

*QUESTION—What are the seven branches of philosophy?*

*Answer*—According to the opinions of the Classical philosophers, the general term "philosophy" embraced seven distinct departments of thought as follows:

METAPHYSICS, the consideration of the superphysical causes that support the world. According to philosophy, all visible things are suspended from invisible causes, the universe itself being merely the visible manifestation of invisible principles. Metaphysics is that department of thought devoted to the discovery and classification of those divine or spiritual energies that are indeed the ever-invisible roots of the Tree of Life.

LOGIC is the discipline of reasonableness. Untrained minds are incapable of determining the truthfulness or fact-value in conflicting systems of thought. To be logical, a fact must arise from a certain source and flow formally to reasonable and consistent conclusions. Logic teaches man to "think things through," and not to accept confused and inconsistent premises merely because he lacks the faculty to compare one opinion with another and determine that which is the most reasonable. The primary rule is the law of Cause and Effect.

ETHICS may be defined as that branch of philosophy which applies the great truths of life to the social relationships of the individual. Ethics is the living of the laws of the philosophic life. No one can be unethical and at the same time wise, for ethics is the certain evidence of inward enlightenment. Ethics lies at the root of civilization, and civilization implies a commonwealth of purpose united upon ethical principles of procedure. Ethics is both behavior and relationship.

PSYCHOLOGY meant to the ancients the science of the soul. It was that part of philosophy which was devoted to the understanding of the subjective part of human consciousness. Psychology involves not only an examination of the eight parts of the soul but also the perfecting of exercises and disciplines by which the soul can be perfected and released from the domination of the animal instincts of the lower nature.

EPISTEMOLOGY is concerned with the subject of knowledge itself. Is it possible for an imperfect creation to possess the capacity to even grasp the import of perfection? Is Truth actually knowable to an imperfect man? The general conclusion in this department has been that man cannot know Absolute Truth, but is capable of realizing an ever-unfolding standard of relative Truth. The finite cannot know the Infinite, but all may perceive better than they do, and by living up to what they perceive, they grow toward the Infinite which lies beyond.

ESTHETICS is the philosophy and science of Beauty. The philosophy of Beauty leads to the inevitable conclusion that The Beautiful is an aspect of the Divine Nature. Beauty is to the soul what food is to the body. The inward man rejoices in the appearance of symmetry, harmony and rhythm. Esthetics as a science cultivates man's love of Beauty through the arts— painting, poetry, music and the dance. These have always been part of religion. One of the duties of religion is to nourish the soul through the cultivation of the esthetic arts.

THEURGY is the seventh and last part of philosophy. It has been called Divine Magic. Under the term are included the most secret metaphysical practices and the deepest philosophical disciplines. Theurgy is the understanding of certain divine procedures whereby the human reason can be lifted up into unity with and participation in the effulgence of Universal Consciousness. It is the end of philosophy that man should know good and be one with God.

*QUESTION—What are the philosophical disciplines referred to by Pythagoras?*

*Answer—*Pythagoras established a philosophical community at Crotona, a Dorian province in Italy, nearly five hundred years before the Christian era. Those entering the community bestowed all their worldly goods upon the school and lived together in spiritual brotherhood. If, for any reason, a member chose to depart from the community, his possessions were returned to him and a headstone was erected in the community cemetery. This was to signify that the departure from the community was equivalent to philosophic death.

Pythagoras taught his disciples that philosophy was not only an occupation for the mind, but a discipline for the body and soul. He imposed certain regulations as indispensable to the development of understanding. These were called the Pythagorean disciplines.

The first of these disciplines was the imposing of a period of silence upon the candidates. No one could be accepted into the inner circle of the Pythagorean school without a probationship of five years. These five years had to be spent in silence— no word to be spoken during that time. After this ordeal had been successfully passed (and over one hundred disciples succeeded in this difficult requirement), the candidate was then able to control his tongue and to think before speaking.

Pythagoras taught that there could be no great improvement of the mind apart from a general improvement of the whole

life. If men were to think better, they should live better, for
no man's thoughts could be higher than the standard of his
action. If a man would think great and noble thoughts, he must
purify and refine his body and soul. In teaching philosophy,
Pythagoras therefore emphasized that education is not a way of
thinking, but a way of living.

The Pythagoreans practiced retrospection in the evening of
each day. This was a discipline of remembrance and analysis of
past action. The disciple examined his every thought and
impulse during the day just passed, estimating its significance
and deeply regretting any unkind or destructive impulse that
had marred the serenity of his living. From this discipline,
arose forethought. Thought should precede action and not follow
it. It is unphilosophical for a man to act first and think afterwards. No word or deed should spring from thoughtlessness.
By retrospection the disciple becomes responsible, recognizing
the importance of his words and deeds.

The Pythagoreans also practiced concentration. They trained
the mind to examine into the causes and results of action, and
particularly they cultivated continuity of thought.

In addition to these mental disciplines, the Pythagoreans
practiced charity and temperance, avoiding the consciousness
of possession and the excesses of the appetites. They encouraged
gentleness and simplicity of manner, and dedicated their lives
to a code of harmoniousness and detachment. The members of
the order were frequently invited to participate in the problems
of politics and in the courts of law. Their judgment was
always impartial and their advice democratic and just. They
believed completely that only those who live the life can know
the doctrine.

*QUESTION—What is the difference between religion and philosophy?*

*Answer*—Religion is satisfied to worship; philosophy seeks to understand. Religions are paths of the heart; philosophies paths of the mind. Emotion is a dominant factor in religion, but plays a small part in philosophy. Religious hysteria is an excess of emotion that finds no place in a philosopher's code. It seldom occurs to the religious person that salvation must be earned. To him belief and acceptance are the foundations of security. Prayer and penance are mighty forces to the religiously minded, but the zealot seldom inquires into the nature of the God to whom he prays and seldom attempts to analyze the efficacy of the penances. By the philosopher, intelligent living is regarded as more efficacious than platitudes and affirmations, and knowledge more virtuous than blind acceptance.

In ancient times religion and philosophy constituted one body of learning. All priests were philosophers and all philosophers were priests. After the decline of Classical civilization, the body of knowledge was divided. Religion and philosophy became separate institutions. Religion was left mindless, and philosophy heartless. The result was the sad dilemma that we find today—blind theologies on the one hand, and materialistic, soulless philosophies on the other.

But the student must differentiate between the morbid, conflicting philosophies of today and the great ideals for which original philosophy stood. For that reason there is little use in studying modern philosophies, nor can modern translations of old philosophies always be trusted. To the metaphysician, philosophy means that sublime department of ancient learning which has been justly called the "science of sciences."

The purpose of philosophy is to discover Truth, to understand Truth, to lift the intellect into final union with the

Ageless Wisdom that sustains the world. This was also the original task of religion. In modern theologies, however, the purposes of religion are obscured and hundreds of petty sects are casting lots for the garments of authority. Religion is purification, philosophy is wisdom; religion is aspiration, philosophy is realization.

In religion man comes to love Truth, and through philosophy, to attain Truth. The beginning of the path is the realization of the reality of things unseen, and the consummation of life is to be one with that sovereign and perfect knowledge which religion has called the "Light of Ages."

*QUESTION—What solution does philosophy offer to the problems of life?*

*Answer*—As a moderator of all extremes, philosophy brings life under the rule of reason. It is not the purpose of philosophy to merely intellectualize living; but rather, through improving the mind, to give each person a perspective sufficient to inspire toward constructive and well-purposed action.

Most of the evils of modern living are rooted in thoughtlessness, rather than actual ignorance. Most people *know* much better than they *do,* but they lack continuity of mental purpose. The mind is the governor of the body. If the mind fails in judgment, the body suffers, and the whole life loses meaning and purpose.

One should not think of philosophy as an abstract science of the ancients, but as an ever-practical guide to the daily decisions of life. Each individual must have some standard within himself to inspire toward the realization of the One, the doing of the Beautiful, and the achievement of the Good. Philosophy, as religion, would bring to an end the conflict of cults and creeds, uniting all men in the worship of one Supreme Principle. Philosophy, as science, would consider not only the diversified phenomena of nature, but would realize that all manifesting things are fragments of one Eternal Being and manifestations of one absolute and sufficient Law. Philosophy, as politics, would bring nations into a rational comradeship of purpose, recognizing individuality, but circumscribing all separate purposes with one universal and sufficient program.

To whatever branch of living and thinking we apply philosophy, there comes deeper realization, greater courage of accomplishment, and a better understanding of that which is necessary and that which can be accomplished. Only the philosopher has the wisdom to understand, the courage to do, and the discretion to accomplish all things in the noblest and most impersonal way.

*QUESTION—Why does this age have so few philosophers?*

*Answer—*While it may not be said that man is entirely a product of his age, it is nevertheless true that environment and opportunity have much to do with molding the outward character of individuals. Man, having within himself numerous talents and abilities, usually manifests those most consistent with his environment. In an age of poets, all men will naturally try to write poetry, and what men try to do they draw out from themselves. In philosophical eras, thinking is a fashion; but in economic eras, thinking is unfashionable and accumulation is the fancy of the day.

Plato explains that philosophical eras are the result of great cycles of time. These cycles he terms a Great Year, explaining that as the ordinary year is made up of spring, summer, autumn, and winter, each with a certain degree of fertility or sterility, so in a Great Year, made up of twenty-five thousand human years, there are similar seasons. In sterile seasons, men turn to material and inferior accomplishments, whereas in fertile seasons philosophers flourish. The most fertile season of each Great Cycle is called the Golden Age, and all men live together in enlightenment. Then there are the Ages of Silver, Bronze and Iron wherein spiritual matters diminish. The mind of man, suffering from the sterility of its world, diminishes in stature until, in the Age of Iron, wars and hatreds destroy the ignorant and the perverse.

But even in sterile seasons there is an occasional exception to the general rule, even as some crops grow in off years. There are some wise with us always. But in sterile seasons, wisdom is the exception, whereas in fertile periods, it is the rule. It is harder to be virtuous and intelligent when this effort is opposed by the whole general trend of society. But in no time is accomplishment actually impossible. Like the ebbing and flowing of the sea, are the alternations of spiritual and material eras. Like day and night, one follows the other. This is an era of darkness, but there is a Light that shines in the darkness for those who can discover it. The path of wisdom is obscured by the night of ignorance, but the sincere carry a light of their own and discover the path in spite of the encircling gloom.

*QUESTION—Is it possible to separate spirituality and wisdom? In other words, can a person be spiritually perfect and yet not possess all knowledge?*

*Answer*—It is not possible to separate spirituality and wisdom. Spirituality actually means that the individual lives or exists upon the level of his spiritual nature, or is possessed by the divinity within him. Divinity can have no ignorance within it.

God cannot lack anything. Therefore, wisdom is an inevitable correlative of complete spiritual development. The difficulty that has arisen and causes this question, lies in the misunderstanding of the nature of spirituality. We are assured in the Scriptures that there is "not one perfect." We know that at this stage of evolution, it is impossible for a human being to be absolutely perfect, either spiritually or physically, for perfection itself is an ultimate, far from our finite state. A person may possess a certain measure of spirituality, but even in the wisest, this measure is hopelessly incomplete. To the same degree that we have spiritual development, we must have an extension of knowledge.

There are certain metaphysical groups that promise "cosmic consciousness" as the result of metaphysical exercises. We have met many people claiming to possess this "cosmic consciousness," but a brief conversation with them clearly indicates that they are suffering from mild hallucination. Cosmic consciousness is all-knowing, and no secret of nature can be concealed from those who possess even a moderate degree of true illumination. Any person claiming to possess cosmic consciousness, and at the same time manifesting all the limitations and imperfections of the flesh, must be suspected of imposture or delusion.

*QUESTION—Give the Philosopher's Creed.*

*Answer*—In his little work titled *Miscellanies,* Mr. Thomas Taylor, the distinguished Platonist, published what he called *The Creed of the Platonic Philosopher.* This Creed is a summary of the whole Orphic Theology as perpetuated by Pythagoras, Plato, and the Alexandrian Neo-Platonists. Speaking of the Platonic philosophy, Mr. Taylor prophesies that it "will again flourish for very extended periods, through all the infinite revolutions of time." The following articles are a summary of the Philosopher's Creed as extracted from the legitimate disciples of the Greek Mysteries:

1. I believe: in one First Cause of all things, whose nature is so immensely transcendent that It cannot be named, spoken of, conceived by opinion, known, or perceived by any being.

2. I believe: that if it be lawful to give a name to That which is Ineffable, the appellations of the *One* and the *Good* are the most adapted to It. The first indicates that It is the Principle of all things, and the second that It is the ultimate object of the desire of all things.

3. I believe: that this immense Principle produced such things as are first and proximate to Itself and most similar to Itself. Hence this Principle produces many principles out of Its own ineffable nature.

4. I believe: that since all things differ from each other and are multiplied, with their proper differences, each of these multitudes is suspended from One proper Principle. Thus, all beautiful things, whether in soul or in body, are suspended from one fountain of beauty, etc.

5. I believe: that such things as are first produced by the One Good are of divine nature most like Itself, whereas those more remotely produced participate in the One Good to a lesser degree, causing the differences in nature.

6. I believe: that all things are transcendently more excellent in the Divine Nature than in their aspect of separation from the Divine Nature.

7. I believe: that the most proper method of venerating this great Principle of Principles is to extend in silence the highest parts of the soul toward it in aspiration and understanding.

8. I believe: that self-subsistent natures are the immediate offspring of this One Principle and may be denominated the Intelligible Gods.

9. I believe: that incorporeal form, or ideas, resident in a Divine Intellect, are the archetypes or models of everything which has subsistence according to Nature.

10. I believe: that this world, depending on its Divine Artificer, is animated by Divine Soul and is justly called by Plato "the blessed God."

11. I believe: that the great body of the world may be properly called a whole, on account of the perpetuity of its duration, though it is nothing more than a flowing eternity.

12. I believe: that all the parts of the universe are unable to participate in the providence of divinity in a similar manner, but that all natures, according to their own essential being, participate in the First Good.

13. I believe: that the world, considered as one great comprehending whole, is a divine animal, possessing in the first place a self-perfect unity by which it becomes a god; in the second place, a divine intellect; in the third place, a divine soul; and in the last place, a deified body.

14. I believe: that after the immense Principle of Principles, a beautiful series of Principles proceeds, all largely partaking of the Ineffable, all stamped with the occult characters of Deity, all possessing an overflowing fulness of Good. That from these dazzling summits, these ineffable blossoms, these divine propagations, being, life, intellect, soul, nature and body depend; *monads* suspended from *unities,* deified natures proceeding from Deity.

15. I believe: that man is a microcosm comprehending in himself *partially* everything which the world contains divinely and *totally.*

16. I believe: that the rational part of man, of which his essence consists, is of a self-motive nature, suspended between intellect and nature.

17. I believe: that the human, as well as every mundane soul, uses periods and restitutions of its proper life. Everything which is moved perpetually, and participates of time, revolves periodically, and proceeds from the same to the same.

18. I believe: that the soul, while an inhabitant of earth, is in a fallen condition, an apostate from Deity, an exile from the orb of Light. And that it can only be restored, while on earth, to the Divine Likeness and be able after death to re-ascend to the intelligible world, by the exercise of the *cathartic* and *theoretic* virtues. The former purifies it from the defilements of the mortal nature, and the latter elevates it to the vision of True Being. Such a soul returns after death to its kindred star from which it fell, and enjoys a blessed life.

19. I believe: that the human soul essentially contains all knowledge, and that whatever knowledge it acquires in the present life, is nothing more than a recovery of what it once possessed, which discipline evokes from its dormant retreat.

20. I believe: that the soul is punished in a future life for the crimes it has committed in the present life; but this punishment is proportioned to the crime and is not perpetual, but is in order that the soul may be restored to its proper perfection.

21. I believe: that the human soul, on its departure from the present life, will, if not properly purified, pass into other bodies until it has perfected itself.

22. I believe: that souls that live according to virtue shall in other respects be happy; and, when separated from the irrational nature and purified from all body, shall be conjoined with the gods, and govern the whole world, together with the Deity by whom it was produced.

# RELIGION

## PART THREE

*QUESTION—What are the religious systems of the world and the keynotes of their teachings?*

*Answer*—The Wisdom Religion, revealed to mankind in the beginning of civilization, is one body of spiritual knowledge. All men are not equally able to receive truth, nor has anyone's interpretation of truth been acceptable to all men. Races are rungs on the ladder of evolution, and to each race has been given of spiritual knowledge as much as was assimilable and applicable. The one wisdom religion, interpreted in the thought and word of the different nations of the world and in the different periods of human progress, has resulted in what we call the world religions—many faiths bearing witness to one faith, many interpretations bearing witness to one eternal truth.

World religions should be divided into living and dead faiths. Living faiths are those functioning through religious organizations in the modern world. Dead faiths are such as belong to the past and play little active part in modern religious thought. It should be remembered, however, that some elements of so-called dead faiths survive in the living religions, so that, in the last analysis, all religious thought lives and influences civilization through all the ages.

Of dead faiths, the Osirian religion of Egypt, the Orphic religion of Greece, the religion of Akhnaton, and the Mysteries of the Central American Indians are examples. In these faiths the sacred books are at least partly lost, the temples have crumbled, the priesthoods have been dispersed, and the laity has followed after other beliefs. The moral force of these lost doctrines has survived, and, particularly in the case of Greek philosophy, profoundly influenced Christianity and Islamism. The principal living religions of the world are as follows:

1. *Zoroastrianism,* the fire worship of the Persians, was founded by Zarathustra Spitama. The principal doctrine is the teaching of the final reconciliation of good and evil and the perfection of man through the mastery of the destructive forces in his own life.

2. *Brahmanism,* the religion of the first Aryans and the principal faith of the Hindus. The Vedic religions are said to have been communicated to mankind by the rishi or saints of the prehistoric world. The principal doctrine of Vedic religion is the achievement of spiritual understanding through universal knowledge and through secret exercises, ceremonies, and rituals.

3. *Buddhism* arose in India in the sixth century B. C. as the most important of all reforms in the Vedic doctrines. Gautama Buddha, the founder of Buddhism, had, as the keynote of his doctrine, the laws of reincarnation and karma and emancipation by detachment.

4. *Confucianism,* the most important of the religions of China, was founded by the philosopher Confucius in the sixth century B. C. The Confucian doctrines particularly stress the moral and social virtues, and have as their goal the production of the Superior Man—an enlightened human being who lives the life of reason.

5. *Taoism,* a mystical religion founded by Lao Tze, a Chinese metaphysician and a contemporary of Confucius, is

called the "obscure faith." Taoism is devoted to extremely abstract metaphysical speculations concerning the nature of Tao, which is both Universal Truth and the way of its attainment.

6. *Judaism,* the religion of the Jews, founded by Moses, was derived from the secret cults of the Egyptians. It is difficult to state with certainty the age of this faith, which is variously placed beween B. C. 2000 and B. C. 1000. The principal doctrine is contained in the Ten Commandments, and the peculiar virtue promulgated is obedience to divine edict.

7. *Christianity,* a faith founded in the first century of the Christian era, upon the doctrines taught by Jesus the Nazarene, a Syrian mystic. Christianity is best summed up in the commandments Jesus gave to his disciples: that they should love God wholeheartedly and their neighbor as themselves. The keynote is distinctly one of service to common need.

8. *Islamism,* a faith founded by the prophet Mohammed in the sixth century of the Christian era. Mohammed, deeply moved by the corruptions arising in the Christian church and the idolatry of his own people, formulated a reformed system of doctrine based largely on Jewish and Christian premises. The keynote of the faith is the unity of God and the teaching that prophets are not incarnations of God but merely messengers.

9. *Lamaism* was brought to Tibet by Padma Sambhava in the eighth century of the Christian era. Lamaism is a form of Buddhism, teaching reincarnation and karma, but also emphasizing the efficacy of magical formulas, mantra, and prayer.

In addition to these there are religio-philosophical systems which we are handling in the question regarding the Mystery Schools, page 119. There are also lesser religious systems, branches of the major systems or indigenous to various nations and races as their folk-lore and primitive cults. This list of religions could be increased to at least fifty, but those given have exercised the widest influence on the living issues of the modern world.

Each of the religions listed included a literal or simple presentation which is commonly called exoteric. This is intended to meet the needs of ordinary persons who desire simple moral codes by which to live. Each of these faiths also has a deeper, more mystical or philosophical doctrine, usually termed esoteric, intended for the priests and for that small group of mankind which desires to devote its entire life to religious and spiritual issues. In many cases, however, in the modern world, the esoteric part of these religions has been neglected, in some cases even forgotten. The work of restoring the Secret Doctrine is now the great task that confronts all students of comparative religion.

*QUESTION—Is theology the same as religion?*

*Answer*—One should distinguish distinctly between the term *theology* and the term *religion*. By theology is meant any organized system of dogma, creed, ceremonial ritual and sacrament constituting an ecclesiasticism. By religion is meant man's urge to venerate the beautiful, serve the good and see God in everything. When a religious system is crystallized into a sect and is segregated from the beliefs of other men, it becomes a theology. The great world teachers brought philosophical and religious revelations that gradually became instituted and established as theological systems.

Man is naturally a religious animal, but he is a theological animal only by so-called heredity and environment. There is only One Religion in the world; but there are many theologies, which have risen up as competitive organizations, each claiming to be holier than the other. Take, for example, Christianity. The Christian creed consists of two commandments: to love God and to love one another. The simple living of these two commandments consitutes Christianity as religion.

In the last nineteen hundred years, hundreds of sects have arisen, many of them greatly complicated and having elaborate systems and statutes of observances. Today we have over two hundred of these in Christendom, all more or less competitive and greatly divided. These are theologies. To the degree that a spiritual revelation is complicated and divided, to that degree it becomes theological. To the degree that it remains simple and united, to that degree it remains religious.

*QUESTION—Can science be reconciled with religion?*

*Answer—*Science and religion were identical in origin, are divided in their present state, and will be united again to become identical in their ultimate. Religion is concerned with the moral values of existence; science with the physical values of existence. Every physical value is the outcome of a moral impulse. The Divine Spirit of religion created the material world of science. In the last analysis, there is no clear line of demarcation where God leaves off and nature begins. Divinity in itself is spirit; Divinity in form is Nature. Religion has become crystallized into theological institutons that maintain themselves, to a great degree, by magnifying points of difference. Science has been crystallized into institutions that have isolated themselves from the arts and ethics of the race and have dedicated their time and effort to exploration and classification of material phenomena.

It will probably be some time before the church and the laboratory will recognize that they are essentially identical. Therefore the only way that we can reconcile science and religion at the present time is in the nature of an enlightened man. A person who has accomplished this reconciliation within himself is properly called a philosopher, because he has recognized that the purpose of all knowledge is to discover God, and that from this discovery must arise, finally, systems of thought dedicated to the perfection of man, through accumulated knowledge. All opposites of learning are reconciled in the soul of the wise man.

*QUESTION—Who wrote the Bible?*

*Answer*—The popular superstition of the last century, that every jot and tittle of the Old and New Testaments were written by the very hand of God, has lost favor with more serious thinkers in the present generation. Research into the antiquities of nations and the origins of sacred books brings a new and more reasonable perspective on the matter of the authors of ancient scriptural books.

Each of the religious systems of the world has preserved collections of inspired writings, sometimes attributed to the founder of the faith and at other times traced to early sages and prophets. The Bibles of the world are an imposing literature, for the most part noble and inspiring works, combining lofty speculations with a certain amount of irrelevant historical, or pseudo-historical, data.

The sacred books of China include the Yih-King, Tao-Teh-King, and the Confucian Analects. Among the Hindus, the Vedas and Puranas occupy chief place in religious literature. The sacred book of the Persians is the Zend-Avesta. The

Mohammedans cherish the Koran. The ancient Greeks revered the Orphic Rhapsodies; and among the Egyptians, an ancient collection of writings called the Book of the Dead was held in peculiar admiration.

In comparison to some of the sacred books, the scriptural writings of the Jews and Christians are of recent date. There can be no question that, in religious matters, races and nations have derived their inspiration from previous cultures and contiguous nations. The Old Testament contains fragments and fables traceable to Hindu, Egyptian, Persian and even Chinese origins. The early parts of Genesis were probably compiled from the records of the Babylonians and Chaldeans. Israel, led into captivity, incorporated into its spiritual tradition elements from Assyrian and Egyptian dogma; and Moses, the law-giver of Israel, was an initiated priest of the Egyptian Mysteries.

Nor is the New Testament free from evidence of compilation. Elements from the life of Bacchus have been woven into the story of Jesus. The Eleusinian, Sabean and Mithraic Mysteries are evident, especially in the Apocalypse. The Christian doctrine was certainly influenced by the Essenes, Nazarenes and Therapeutic sects, now believed to have been of Grecian origin. The early fathers of the Church, in their interpretations of Christian mysticism, also drew heavily upon Gnostic lore, of Syrian and Egyptian origin, and from the opinions of the Alexandrian School.

In substance, then, we may say that the sacred writings of the Jews and Christians, like other sacred books of the world, are compilations of tradition, mystical lore, and mythical history. The New Testament makes the greatest claim for historical accuracy, but even in the Gospels themselves, many sources of information are drawn upon.

The Bible, often called the Drama of the Ages, is just that. The rudiments of it were brought into new lands by migrating peoples. The roots of Scripture are deep in the soil of Asia, and the Aryan migrations spread the old lore over the whole face of the earth. Nations developed and specialized their own traditions, building up their sacred books and histories; but in every case, deeply hidden under diverse interpretations, the same story is told, the same commandments are given, the same virtues are emphasized. Like morality and honesty, religious tradition belongs to no one people, but is distributed somewhat evenly over the whole face of the earth.

According to Eastern philosophers, the religious institutions of mankind were given to the world by seven sacred sages, known as the Rishi, whose memory is preserved through the symbolism of the seven stars of the Little Bear, the constellation that guards the pole. These Sages lived in the antediluvian time, bringing to man the divine wisdom from previous worlds and previous rounds of evolution. It is said that the Aryan Scripture, or rather the Aryan interpretation of the great spiritual institutions, was given to the race by a great soul known in India as Vaivasvata-Manu. The revelation was made over a million years ago while the Aryans still dwelt together in the high plateaus of the Himalaya mountains.

With the birth of each new race, a new interpretation of religion is given. Sacred books are built up about this interpretation, but in every case the interpretation is merely a restatement of ever-existing facts. The restatement becomes the keynote of the religious purpose of racial unfoldment.

*QUESTION—What is the Trinity?*

*Answer*—Nearly all the great religious systems of the world represent their supreme Deity as manifesting through a trinity or triad of attributes. The origin of the doctrine of the trinity is too remote to permit of discovery and analysis, but the belief that universal energy manifests triadically appears to be justified by the findings of modern science. Deity was frequently symbolized by the ancients as an equilateral triangle. Pythagoras represented Divinity under the form of a triangle of dots to signify the Divine Power and its extensions or manifestations. In India, the trinity consists of the creative, preservative and disintegrative aspects of Universal Life. These powers are represented by three human faces united in one head—as in the Trimurti of Elephanta—this composite figure representing the triple mystery of the Godhead. In Christianity, the Father, Son and Holy Ghost are the three persons of the trinity or triform-unity. The three divine powers emanate from themselves the three worlds or planes of existence, which Christian theology terms heaven, earth, and hell; or in the terms of Platonic philosophy, the spiritual, intellectual and material creation. In the old Mysteries, the three powers of the creative triad are called will, wisdom, and action—or consciousness, intelligence, and force. These powers are sometimes represented as three pillars or columns, as in the case of the Cabala. These pillars are referred to as the triple foundation of the world, and represent the three forms of Universal Energy by which the equilibrium of creation is preserved.

*QUESTION—Who was Christ?*

*Answer*—The principal sources of information concerning the life of Jesus the Christ are the four so-called gospels.

In addition to these records, there are apocryphal gospels, still regarded as uncanonical, containing fragments of history, and some material evidently legendary. The Jewish Talmud mentions a Jesus who preached in Nazareth and Galilee, and was stoned to death for his heresies. It would seem, however, that the Jesus of the Talmud (Jehoshua) lived about 100 B. C. The writings of the ante-Nicene fathers contain some traditions presumably derived from first-century sources. The most important of the ante-Nicene records are found in Irenaeus. There is a brief statement in Josephus, but this is regarded by most authors as a forgery.

Fragmentary mention of Jesus is to be found in many third- and fourth-century Christian documents, but he is ignored by all the important historians of his time. Taking all in all, the gospels remain as the only systematic exposition of his life and works. The most important records, besides the gospels, are the Gnostic writings; but in these Christ is treated as symbolical rather than historical, and they are not contemporary.

The average modern Christian does not realize that the fathers of the early Church recognized a difference between Jesus and Christ. Jesus was the Nazarene adept whose illumination is said to have occurred at the time of his baptism by John. The Christos is the spirit of Universal Truth, and to be "christened" means to be illumined or to have opened the inward faculties of realization. Jesus the christened, or Jesus the Christ, therefore means Jesus the enlightened or the one upon whom the Spirit of Truth has descended. There is a perfect parallel in the story of Buddha. The young prince of India was named Gautama Siddhartha. Under the Bodhi-tree he received the Illumination. The Spirit of Truth, "Buddhi," which is universal wisdom, descended upon him, or, more correctly, was released out of his own nature. He then became Gautama Buddha—Gautama the Enlightened.

When Jesus said that the Father was in him, he did not mean that the Sovereign Creator of the universe had become solely and entirely incarnate within a man; nor did he mean that the Universal Principle of all things was not in other creatures. What he actually meant was the mystical statement that through realization, he had come to the understanding of his own at-one-ment with Truth, or universal Reality.

The term *Christian* should therefore be limited to one who has received the inner light, and should not be bestowed upon the congregation of any theological movement. A man is not a Christian until Christ is born in him, or more literally, until wisdom, virtue, integrity, and understanding are perfected in his own nature.

*QUESTION—Are miracles possible, and did Christ perform miracles?*

*Answer—*The answer to this question depends upon the interpretation we place upon the word *miracle.* If we think of a miracle as a truly miraculous circumstance, contrary to all the laws of nature and performed by means of a special dispensation, we must answer in the negative. If, on the other hand, we acknowledge that certain highly evolved persons are capable of performing certain extraordinary feats beyond our comprehension, but nevertheless in harmony with the laws of nature, then we can answer in the affirmative.

According to Paracelsus, "The beginning of wisdom is the beginning of supernatural power." Man, exploring the mysteries of the universe, discovers, through consecrated and enlightened effort, secrets that are unknown to the average mortal. The instruction of the mind, purification of the body, and dedication of the life to high purpose releases in man energies and powers by which what appears to be the miraculous is accomplished.

Miracles are reported of many great saints and sages in all periods of history. The priests of the ancient temples healed sickness by means of prayers and invocations; and the same procedure—called among primitive people Shamanism—still prevails throughout Asia.

Miracles are reported of such great men as Pythagoras, Buddha, Appollonius of Tyana, and Albertus Magus. The healings accomplished by Paracelsus caused him to be accused of practicing sorcery, and similar reports were circulated in the case of Henry Cornelius Agrippa. So-called miracles frequently occurred in the life of Madame Blavatsky, as recently as the last half of the 19th century. The miraculous is recorded in the philosophy of every people, and he who would question the supernatural opposes a monument of evidence.

There is nothing recorded in the miracles of Jesus that could not be performed by an adept in the occult arts; and, according to the old records, Jesus was an Essene adept versed in the mysteries of the Egyptians and of the secret societies of Syria and the Lebanon. It is quite possible that some of the accounts of the wonders performed by Jesus are apocryphal, interpolated into the Gospels and Epistles to increase the prestige of the early Church. This, however, is apart from our point. Whether he performed miracles or not is a subject for controversy, but his ability to perform them as an Essene initiate cannot be questioned.

In India today, superphysical and apparently miraculous feats are constantly being performed. Highly trained Yogis can levitate themselves, walk upon lakes and streams, or travel instantly from one place to another, by the special training and disciplining of their lives. The reason miracles are out of fashion in the Western world is that they are part of an ascetic code of living. They result from a highly developed mystical philosophy. Adepts of such philosophy are rare to the Western world, which is far more concerned with accumulation of material things than with the unfoldment of the spiritual nature.

*QUESTION—What is meant by the Holy Ghost?*

*Answer*—All the great wisdom religions of the world agree that the Great Causal Energy which we term God manifests throughout creation as a triune or triform energy. Among the Brahmans, the Supreme Deity is represented with three faces, and its aspects are designated Brahma the Creator, Vishnu the Preserver, and Shiva the Destroyer. In Greece, the triad consists of Phanes, Chronos, and Zeus; and in Christendom, the divine attributes are called the Father, Son, and Holy Ghost. These three manifestations represent God as spirit (the Father), God as soul, or mind (the Son), and God as body, or activity (the Holy Ghost).

In the esoteric system of the Gnostics, the Holy Ghost was the vast Active Principle which ensouls the material creation. It was termed the *Demiurgus,* and is the source of those natural laws by which the economy of physical function is preserved. The Holy Ghost of Christendom corresponds very closely to what the pagans called *Nature*—a term that even now is popularly personified, so that we say Mother Nature —regarding nature as the common parent of all material forms. In Egypt, Mother Nature is represented by Isis, who carries in her arms Horus the Christ-child, to signify that soul or mind arises from, or is born through, the experiences of natural existence. This is the interpretation of the statement that

Christ, the Messianic soul, is conceived of the Holy Ghost, or arises from the mystery of nature.

The word *ghost* is from *gast,* or a breath. Holy Ghost means sacred breath. This is a symbolical term referring to the breath of life in all things. When the Creative Process formed the world, as described in Genesis, it sent forth its breath into its creations; and when they received the breath of life, these creatures became living things.

*QUESTION—What is the purpose of baptism?*

*Answer—*The sacrament of baptism descended to Christendom from the old pagan Mysteries, where it was originally a symbol of purification through water, or the cleansing of the body prior to the entrance into a holy place. In the Tabernacle Mysteries of the Jews, there was a great laver of purification in the courtyard, wherein the priests bathed themselves before donning the vestments of sanctity. Even to this day, the Mohammedan mosques have in their courtyards large tanks of water, like pools, wherein the faithful must wash their feet before participating in the services.

The Egyptians recognized two symbolical baptisms: the first of water, symbolizing the purification of the body through strict observance and physical regeneration; the second of fire, symbolizing the enlightenment of the spirit or the descent of consciousness. These baptisms are mentioned in the Gospels. Baptism is a purely symbolical sacrament, a constant reminder that only the pure and the clean are worthy to enter into the knowledge of God.

The literal acceptance of baptism as a method of washing out original sin is purely theological. The original sin is ignorance, which must be washed out, or the body purified therefrom, by the disciplines of wisdom. Truth purifies the life and fits the one who possesses it to enter into the inner sanctuary of the Mystery temple. All the sacraments are similarly symbolical, having no virtue apart from a course of action which they imply. Baptism should always be regarded as the sacrament of self-purification by means of right thinking, right emotion, and right action.

*QUESTION—What is meant by the Resurrection?*

*Answer*—The doctrine of a physical or literal resurrection of the dead, if not peculiar to the Christian church, certainly receives extraordinary emphasis among the denominations of Christendom. It is recorded that many of the early converts believed so firmly that they would reinhabit their bodies at the Last Judgment, that they took extreme means to preserve the mortal remains. In this attitude, the early Christians exceeded even the Egyptians. They did not mummify their dead, but preserved the bodies in oil without removing the viscera.

From a philosophical standpoint, the doctrine of the Resurrection is summed up in Plato's doctrine that the body is the sepulchre of the soul. The account of the Resurrection, so familiar to the pious Christian mind of past centuries, is entirely allegorical. The dust of ages shall not rise again, and all the wisdom of the heavenly host could scarcely reassemble the scattered bones of that innumerable multitude that has gone down to the earth in sleep. If, however, we acknowledge that the body of man is composed of the earth, and that the spirit of man is locked into the body, then we can correctly comprehend the mystery of death. The outward body and the material nature are the graves of the Divine Principle.

The ignorant man imprisons a luminous nature within his unresponsive personality. Ignorance is death; wisdom is life. Enlightenment is release. The wise man only is free. By the Resurrection, therefore, we are to understand enlightenment ascending out of ignorance, the Truth within liberated to manifest through a dedicated and purified body. When man overcomes his appetites, masters his animal impulses, perfects and redeems his heart and mind from their addictions to destructive or illusionary concerns—this is the Resurrection; Truth born out of error, security rising from insecurity, God rising from the earth.

The Resurrection is accomplished through reincarnation. After many lives in the darkness of spiritual obscuration, each man ascends to the Light. The "stone is rolled away," and what is the stone but materiality? As Lazarus came forth from the tomb, so in the end each human soul comes forth from its ages of blindness and doubt to take its place among the enlightened. The soul in every man, his own Higher Self, is the Resurrection and the Life, and who so perfects his soul shall come forth out of darkness and dwell in the Light.

*QUESTION—Please explain religious hysteria, so often seen at evangelical meetings.*

*Answer—*Religious hysteria plays an important part in many of the world's theological systems. From the Shamanism of primitive cults to such elaborate religious institutions as Christianity, hysteria is an important equation in the phenomenon of faith. Most people of devout religious leaning are intensely emotional. Orthodox theology is for the most part a faith of inhibitions. For many hundreds of years, it was regarded as a theological sin to be comfortable, and to be happy endangered the immortality of the soul.

A creed that constantly preached "thou shalt not," and constantly limited the normal emotional expression of its followers, was certain to bring a goodly number of its parishioners to a state of psycho-emotional hysteria. Imagination stimulating emotion must result in emotional crisis. Of course, people rolling on the floor are not filled with the Holy Spirit, nor are they under the power of God. They are simply in an emotional spasm and have lost all semblance of self-control. These spasms are very detrimental to the bodily harmony, and a person who too frequently gives way to them destroys emotional poise and mental balance. It is incredible that in this enlightened century, the most primitive and barbaric forms of religious sorcery should still be widely practiced under the name of Christianity.

*QUESTION—What religious training is advisable for children?*

*Answer*—Small children, too young to understand any of the philosophical truths of life, are best taught by beautiful example of enlightened living in the home. As the child becomes a little older, it can be taught that religion means, first of all, living beautifully and nobly, and that a beautiful life is the most acceptable offering to the God of Truth and Beauty dwelling in all parts of the universe. Under existing conditions, we would recommend that the spiritual education of the child remain as a sacred duty of the parent; for there are no organizations at the present time that can compare with enlightened parental influence.

As the child grows older, it should also be taught that religion is an inner relationship between the person and the Spirit that dwells in its own heart. No special sectarian religious training should be given to the child. If in later years the child, grown up to mature judgment, chooses to affiliate with some religious movement, that choice should result from mature judgment and not from parental influence. It is a tragedy to set a child's mind in any theological rut before the child has sufficient individuality to resist this influence and choose its own course of action.

# LIFE AND DEATH

## PART FOUR

*QUESTION—What is the doctrine of reincarnation and karma?*

*Answer*—Reincarnation and karma are the principal doctrines of Buddhism that were also taught by several other systems of esoteric philosophy, especially the Pythagorean and Platonic schools. The doctrine of reincarnation teaches that man lives on this earth not once, but many times, returning until he has perfected himself in every lesson that this world has to teach.

The doctrine of karma teaches that everything that happens in nature is dominated by the law of cause and effect. The law of cause and effect applied to man shows that everything that happens to an individual is an aspect of universal justice. Every man is in the place he has earned for himself; every man is doing the thing he has earned the right to do; no one is suffering for the mistakes of others, but for his own mistakes. The only way to be happy, therefore, is to live well, thus setting in action constructive cycles of cause and effect. If we want to be wise, we must earn wisdom. Every individual who lives in the world is in the place he has earned for himself by his actions in this or previous lives.

The average number of earth lives through which the human soul will pass in this cycle of evolution is approximately eight hundred. By the time man has lived in this world eight hundred times, he will know how to live well. Reincarnation makes accomplishment possible to all, and makes each man the captain of his own soul. The doctrines of vicarious atonement and infant damnation are disposed of forever. Man lives in an honest world, in which he can succeed only by being honest himself. The doctrine of reincarnation and karma is the only teaching concerning the reasons for existence and the ultimate goal of life, that is worthy of a philosopher.

*QUESTION—What is death?*

*Answer*—Metaphysically interpreted, death is the separation of the higher and lower principles in man. The living human being is a compound creature consisting of superphysical principles manifesting through a physical body composed of the elements of so-called physical nature. The superphysical principles constitute the real living person, and the body is merely a vehicle by means of which the superphysical man can manifest in this physical world. The spiritual self dwells in the body, like a man living in a house, but the average person never learns that the house is not the man, or that there is any difference between the two. Plato says that man lives in his body, like the oyster lives in his shell, and the Hindu philosophers refer to the body as the garment or vestment of the superphysical self.

By means of the nerve centers and the ductless gland system, the spiritual man controls and directs the physical body, giving it the appearance of life. Thus it is not really the body that causes animation, but the spiritual man in the body. The light of the inner self shines out through the body, like the flame shining through the glass of a lantern. There is just as much difference between the qualities of the inner man and his outer body, as there is between the flame in the lamp and the glass and metal that form the lantern.

In the symbolism of the Greek philosophers, it was said that the body is the temporary house of the inner self. The real spiritual man is like a traveler wandering across the desert of living. This inner self stays for a while in one house and then departs from the house and journeys on to another one. Each time the ego builds a house, it builds a better one, or, as the Persian poets wrote, weaves ever more beautiful garments for itself out of the wealth, beauty, and understanding of the inner soul. After the entity has dwelt in a body for a certain number of years, the body, which is ruled by the laws of the physical world, grows old and decrepit and unworthy of the life within. When the life can no longer function because of disease, accident, or the natural infirmities of age, the ego departs from the body, producing by its departure the phenomenon of death.

Death is not the dying of the self, or the ceasing of the spirit, or even the ceasing of the purpose of the spirit; it is rather life, with mind, soul, and understanding departing from a worn-out garment or a house no longer fit for its inhabitance. Plato says that the spirit rises from the sepulchre of the body. The Bhagavad-Gita, the beautiful mystical book of the Brahmans, says that the spirit casts off its worn-out garments and prepares itself a more glorious vestment.

The corpse is really the natural condition of the body, and in death we perceive the earthy elements returned to the inanimate state. The body is therefore like an empty glove from which the hand has been withdrawn. But because we see the empty glove, we have no proof that the hand is also dead. Because we see the empty shells by the side of the sea, we are apt to think all life ends at the grave. But life never dies. Bodies cease, but life is eternal. Death is the spirit casting off the bonds of flesh, to function for a time in the invisible world before building another vehicle of physical manifestation. Thus while death seems to the uninformed to be a great tragedy, it is understood by the philosopher as a magnificent spiritual experience, life's supreme adventure—the return of the spirit to its own state, and a release of inner greatness from bondage to the limitations of inadequate flesh.

*QUESTION—Describe the after-death state.*

*Answer*—During the years of life in the physical world, man gathers a vast amount of experience. During life this experience is not digested nor arranged in any systematic pattern. The period between incarnations is the period of assimilation, during which the entity builds the experiences of life into the soul nature, to become internal strength. The entity does not make any new development or growth between lives, for its subjective existence does not extend into the sphere of phenomena.

The after-death state is variously symbolized in the different religious systems of the world. Divested of symbolical figures, the state of life between incarnations may be summed up as follows:

After leaving the physical body, the entity functions temporarily in the etheric double, or body of the fifth element. This body resembles closely the appearance of the physical form, but is composed of subtle superphysical essences. The entity remains in this body only a few days unless it is earthbound or is a suicide. In the former case, it will remain until its tie with the world is broken; and in the latter, it will remain until the time its normal death would have occurred. The consciousness in the etheric body is almost identical with physical consciousness, and those who have passed on are frequently not even aware that they have died. The etheric double is really a part of the physical body, and after the entity has passed on to the inner planes of nature the etheric body slowly disintegrates, retaining for some time its form and constituting what is sometimes called the ghost. These etheric forms are the ghosts that sensitive people often see about graveyards.

After a brief period in the etheric double, the entity passes on to the astral world, the sphere of desires and emotions, and functions in the astral body, leaving the etheric shell to disintegrate in the etheric world. The astral world is called the sphere of punishments and rewards. In this plane, the entity experiences as fact the emotional reflexes of its physical living. The ancients say that the principal thing about this experiencing is that by some mysterious law of nature, the entity becomes the victim of all evils it has committed. This period of correction is called by the Roman Church *Purgatory,* or the place of purging from sin. It is the sphere where man puts his emotional life in order and builds the nucleus for a future emotional nature. Having worn out the records in the sin-body, the entity passes on to the highest sphere of the emotional world, where its constructive emotions build esthetic values into the permanent consciousness. Having lived through constructive emotions and gained from them their full merit, the entity then moves out of the astral body and functions in its mental nature.

The mental body is the sphere of thought. It is likewise divided into destructive and constructive planes. After the lower mind has been expiated and its records built into consciousness, the entity functions in the higher or constructive mind, where the rewards of right mental action become the nucleus of greater mental integrity in the next life. Having completed its mental function in the sphere and substance of mind, the entity passes out of the mental and remains in suspension, without function and without awareness, for a certain time before it begins the building of a new chain of bodies for its next life.

The cycle of after-death experience differs with different grades of evolution. Primitive peoples, having but little individuality, have but little after-death experience, and reincarnate almost immediately. Average entities of the fifth root race are out of incarnation from eight hundred to twelve hundred years. The length of time in the planes of the astral and mental spheres depends upon the intensity of the feeling and thinking and the scope of the records that have been accumulated during earth life. Very highly advanced souls are out of incarnation for many thousands of years, and, because of the depth of their thinking, have extended periods of consciousness in the mental plane.

The children who die before reaching adolescence usually reincarnate almost immediately, as do also animals, because there are no important records to be built into the egoic consciousness. There is no absolutely set interval between incarnations, but usually the intervals are reasonably regular, and there is an alternation of sex. This is the philosophical doctrine, which disposes of heaven and hell by teaching that these terms signify the after-death cycles of reward and punishment. There is no eternal damnation in philosophy, and no static heaven. There is infinite growth through cycles of experience which men call life and death.

*QUESTION—Explain the process of rebirth?*

*Answer—*Rebirth is the descent of the superphysical man into the elements of the material world. The ancients signified this process under the symbolism of souls ascending and descending the rungs of a great ladder that extended from heaven to earth. The Eleusinian Mysteries, which were celebrated for more than a thousand years in Attica, consisted of nine symbolical pageantries to represent the nine conditions passed through by the soul as it departed from its celestial home to take up dwelling in the mortal frame.

The rebirth cycle was represented among the Chaldeans by the myth of Ishtar. This goddess descended through seven gates, leaving with the keepers of the gates the seven emblems of her royalty. At last, bereft of all her grandeurs, she entered the house of Sin, the Moon-god, or as the Greeks expressed it, entered the sublunary sphere. In the kingdom of Sin, Ishtar was tortured and humiliated. All manner of evil was heaped upon her. By this was represented the state of the soul in the physical world. Ishtar was eventually rescued from the god of darkness and, ascending the ladder of the spheres, received back from the custodians the emblems of her divinity. By this is to be understood the restoration of the soul to its state of glory through the disciplines of philosophy.

According to Plato, the human soul is drawn back into the world by the worldliness within itself; that is, the soul, having accepted the reality of material things, is moved by its own conviction back into the sphere of its belief. As worldliness dies within the consciousness, the gravitational pull of matter lessens until at last, released from all the illusions of the material state, the soul ascends from body to union with the blessed gods.

The law that pulls the spiritual entity back to physical life is karma. All causes that have been set up in the physical world must be finished or worked out by physical experience. Man, bound to the generating plane by sense, emotion, feeling, desire and appetite, must conquer these impulses and instincts before the cycle of physical rebirth can end. As Buddha taught, the Nirvana or liberation is accomplished only by the dying out of the fires of emotion and sense in the self. The Greeks represented the soul as naturally yearning upward to the light of Truth, but constantly drawn downward against its will by the imperfection of its lower extremities. The sphinx with the human head and the body of the animal is thus a symbol of the soul. Persephone, whose life is divided between a celestial and infernal abode, is also a figure representing this fact. The parable of the prodigal son who leaves his father's house for the flesh-pots of Egypt, to return in the end repentant, is the Biblical equivalent of the allegories of the Greeks.

Having incorporated into its consciousness the experiences of the previous incarnation, the soul is a compound of experience and karma. Some things have been mastered; much more remains to be accomplished; and the soul is drawn irresistibly back to the sphere of its unfinished labors.

Descending from its own supersubstantial essence, the soul builds around itself an intellectual nature or mental body. Then the soul, robed in its mental vestments and partly obscured by the limitations of thought, descends into the sphere of feeling, where it takes upon itself a body of desire, which further limits its effulgence. Robed in its thoughts and desires, the soul then descends into the sea of the humidic ethers, which the Greeks describe as the link between the visible and invisible worlds. This humidic ether is the sea of life over which rules Poseidon, or Neptune, whose trident is the pitchfork of Satan by which the Prince of evil is said to herd souls in the lower world. The ethers are called also the water of forgetfulness, the ever-flowing spring of Lethe. Immersed in the ethers, the soul forgets its divine estate, and its eyes are closed to the glory of its own source. It is from the ethers that the soul descends into physical form. In the Greek fables, souls waiting to enter physical generation are described as flocks of sheep, and Hermes is their lord. He is called the Psychopomp or the Herder of Souls. Here this god represents cosmic law, especially in the aspects of rein-carnation and karma, the force that brings each human being into physical life in an environment appropriate to its own needs.

By the laws of physical nature, bodies are engendered in the material world. The soul is allotted to a body according to its merits, and flows into the form at the time of quicken-ing. From the time of quickening to the time of birth, the superphysical principles are gradually gaining control of the physical body. At birth the composite entity is launched into individual existence. Through the periods of growth, the soul releases certain of its powers through the body into objective manifestation. The physical principle is released at birth, the vital principle is released at approximately the seventh year, the emotional principle is released at the fourteenth year, and the mental principle at the twenty-first year. The soul, therefore, at the maturity of its physical body, has manifested its subjective bodies through appropriate objective propensities.

Life then continues until the pattern is broken up, either by the accident of death or the intention of philosophy. The wise man grows out of bodies during life, but the uninformed man is violently precipitated out of the body by the disintegra-tion of the physical form.

*QUESTION—Can we communicate with the dead, and is it right to do so?*

*Answer*—Pythagoras of Crotona, one of the greatest of the Greek adepts, taught his disciples that it was possible for the living to communicate with the dead. He warned them, however, against cultivating the art of necromancy, because it accomplished no constructive or useful purpose. Spiritualism attracts to its ranks principally the lonely and bereaved. While there can be no reasonable doubt that a certain percentage of psychical phenomena is genuine, those who give themselves to mediumship and other forms of psychism are greatly victimized through their faith and credulity.

To turn for advice to the dead, is to be unphilosophical. Those who have passed out of this life are no better fitted to advise the living than those still functioning in this world. Nor should the living cling desparately to their friends and relatives who have passed out of this sphere. It may require more of courage to release the dead from our attachments, but to let go is best for all concerned.

There are mysteries in the psychical world that few mortals understand, and he who dabbles with the subtle forces of the unseen universe is apt to repent his audacity. The majority of messages that come from behind the veil are vague, platitudinous and ambiguous; nor is deception unusual. Many lives have been ruined by psychic vagaries. He who listens too often to the whisperings of the "spirits" may find his angels to be demons in disguise. I know personally many lives that have been hopelessly ruined by dabblings in the mediumistic arts. Humanity understands but imperfectly the mysterious forces dwelling in the borderland between the living and the dead. Until man understands more, he should leave alone these forces which may only lead to madness.

The ouija-board, or planchette, called in Europe the devil's flat-iron, and driven from most of the civilized countries of the world, is a psychic toy that has contributed many tragedies to man's mortal state. Automatic writing, a weird, fascinating pastime, may end in a wide variety of disasters. Addiction to psychic practices sets corrosive forces to work in the mind and soul, and all who seek wisdom in its highest and truest form must avoid the blind alley of psychism. Eliphas Levi, the great French magician, said that the astral sphere is a beautiful garden of illusions filled with many rare and scented flowers; that around the stem of every flower is coiled a poisonous serpent, and he who would pluck the blossom receives the sting of death.

The wise student will acknowledge the reality of psychical phenomena. He will admit communication between the worlds is possible, but he will also maintain that psychic things are not for him. He desires not communication with ghosts, nor to be ruled by disembodied voices, nor to seek for truth in a crystal ball. The true path of wisdom is the building of truth and strength within, through study and experience. This simple, positive process needs no assistance from the larvae of the elemental world.

*QUESTION—Can we remember past lives?*

*Answer*—To most people the wisdom of the universe mercifully obscures the past so that the failings and mistakes of other ages shall not overshadow and hinder the present struggle for accomplishment. Under normal conditions, therefore, it is not possible to remember the details of past incarnations. But the power to rescue this memory from the subconscious mind can be developed with the aid of certain special disciplines known to the adepts of the occult sciences. Usually, however, the remembrance of past lives can accomplish no particular good, and time spent in an effort to stimulate this faculty is love's labor lost. It is far more important to devote thought to the improvement of the present condition than to the vain hope of finding some greatness in the past.

There is a certain class of neo-metaphysicians who spend much time discussing their previous incarnations. Strangely enough, most of them believe that in the distant past they were great persons; but in their present lives, they have accomplished nothing and there is not the slightest aura of greatness about them. Such revelations, in which someone remembers that he was Hypatia, Cleopatra, or Napoleon, are indeed old wives' tales not to be taken seriously, but to be included among the hallucinations of physical unbalance, or just plain "fibbing."

The best way for the average person to measure what he has been in the past life is to examine the qualities he brings with him into this life. Each person has special abilities, interests and indifferences, likes and dislikes, tastes and aversions. All these characteristics are the records of what has been experienced in the past. Genius is the present evidence of past effort. All that man is today is the sum of what he has been. The debts man pays today, he incurred yesterday. What is called this life is just a small, visible part of the ages, the epilogue to the drama of yesterday. Most people will find that their past life comes to them in their present incarnation chiefly as unfinished business. Also, as each person goes down the years, flashes of the past come to him. He meets someone whom he has known before. He stands in some place where he knows he has stood before. He reads a book about some past civilization and feels that he has lived and labored in that very age the book describes. If you study your face in the mirror, you may discover in your features the shadow of some ancient race. As you go about the daily labors of life, there is about each thing you do some feeling that it has been done before, some sense of large universals overshadowing the small things of the day. The memory of the past is obscured, but the veil is sometimes very thin, and there are moments in the life of every individual when light shines through and he realizes his kinship with all times and all places.

*QUESTION—If we do not develop spiritually in this life sufficiently to remember our past lives, do we automatically come into possession of this remembrance when we reach the astral world ofter death?*

*Answer*—The transition between the material state and the after-death condition does not bring with it any major improvement in the degree of our knowledge or understanding. The astral body, in which we function after the decease of the physical organism, is not the depository of the records of the past karma. These records are preserved in the ego itself. The transition termed death, while it demonstrates to the individual himself the fact of immortality, does not necessarily bring any broadened viewpoint on the fact of reincarnation and karma. Thus, spirit mediums seldom receive any instruction concerning rebirth from the decarnate entities that speak through them. The memory of past lives comes to the individual only when he has reached a state of development by which the secrets that are locked in the consciousness itself are released into the sphere of objective thinking and knowing. The memory of past lives is locked within the super-conscious self. This self is not released by merely dying, but by the philosophical mystery commonly termed illumination.

*QUESTION—What part does nationality play in reincarnation? Does a person incarnate into a different nation each time he is reborn?*

*Answer*—For practical purposes, we may regard nations as parts of races. They are rungs in the ladder of racial evolution. Nations offer specialized environments for the lives evolving within a racial consciousness. The nation into which an individual is born is determined by evolution and karma. The ego is not necessarily reborn each time into a different nation; it often requires many lives to outgrow national environments, and national consciousness can hold egos to national programs for several lives. The present tendency toward internationalism is reflected in the short lives of nations. Whereas ancient national institutions existed for thousands of years, few nations today retain their essential characteristics for more than from three hundred to five hundred years. This itself is an indication of the speeding up of evolution, a tendency consistent throughout nature. As consciousness unfolds, nationalism must give way to internationalism, and evolution itself will finally bring about the condition of men living together in equity and peace.

*QUESTION—Can we control the length of time between incarnations or determine in advance what the next incarnation shall be?*

*Answer*—Until an entity reaches a very high degree of spiritual development, it does not have the power to control the intervals between incarnations. These intervals, like all other occurrences, arise from karma. The only way in which these intervals can be influenced is by intensity of action, particularly mental action. We do not mean a mental effort to influence the time and condition of rebirth, but rather, the general intensity of mental awareness. The more highly evolved the intellectual nature, the more profound and philosophic the thought, and the greater the scope of judgment, the longer will be the intervals between lives. This arises from the time required by the ego to assimilate into the soul nature the panorama of mental experiences while on earth. Thus, the average individual can transmute the fruits of his mental activity into soul powers in a few hundred years of after-death consciousness, but it is estimated that it will require ten thousand years for Plato to accomplish this, so great was his intellect. Therefore, unless Plato, being a very highly evolved soul, exercises his privilege as an adept to return sooner in the capacity of a teacher, he will normally remain out of incarnation for that length of time.

As to the conditions of a future life, these cannot be directly influenced by the average person, because the next incarnation may be devoted to working out the karma of the present life, or it may be dedicated to the transmutation of karma brought forward from earlier incarnations but not included in the program of the present life. The whole future depends upon the increasing intelligence and integrity of present action.

QUESTION—Do disembodied spirits retain a memory of their earth-life experiences?

Answer—The simple experiments of spiritualism have demonstrated the continuity of consciousness beyond the grave, and all clairvoyants agree that a person who has passed from this state to the subjective plane retains the same identity and individuality as during physical life. A man has four bodies making up what is termed the chain of his personality. The lowest of these bodies is chemical organism. After physical death, the individual functions briefly in his etheric double, or vital body, which also dies, never surviving for any considerable time the disintegration of the physical organism. Under normal conditions, at this stage of our evolution, the average person functions for nearly a thousand years in the astral body. For this entire period, he retains the individuality of his previous incarnation. The astral body is then dissipated by a phenomenon resembling death, and the consciousness is posited in its two-fold mental organism, in which it functions for a period of time consistent with its mental development.

With the disintegration of the mental body, usually some twelve hundred years after death, the entity loses its personality and becomes again a pure, spiritual principle. From this time, the memory of the past life exists only subjectively and the continuity of consciousness is broken. Therefore, after the disintegration of the mental organism, the personality ends as such. This period is followed immediately by preparations within the ego itself for rebirth, when it causes a new personality to emerge out of its own potential creative power. There are some exceptions to this rule due to special developments, and very highly evolved entities will retain individual consciousness for a much greater time.

We should remember that it is not the personality that really grows; it is the ego, or inner self, growing through personality and using personality for the accomplishment of its own ends. Thus John Doe as a personality does not grow through the ages; rather, the eternal self, or the spirit, causes a personality temporarily known as John Doe to be emanated out of itself. At the end of approximately twelve hundred years, John Doe is entirely reabsorbed into the spiritual cause from which it came. John Doe then absolutely ceases, but the experiences and characteristics of John Doe are incorporated into the consciousness of the permanent ego. Personalities are not reborn, but the principles behind personalities are constantly projecting personal organisms out of themselves, and through these personal organisms contacting the experience spheres of life.

*QUESTION—Can past karma be escaped by present good deeds?*

*Answer—*According to the ancient wisdom, that which is done cannot be undone. No philosophical system worthy of the name would fall into the fallacy of vicarious atonement. Nature's bookkeeping system has in it no place for erasures. The motive behind present good deeds should never be to escape past karma, but rather, to prevent the making of more evil karma. An individual whose present life is filled with efforts to improve character and increase the measure of meritorious action, is establishing a solid philosophical foundation of well-being to be enjoyed in future existences. This explains a mystery that confuses many students. A person will say: "All my life I have done good to others, and all my life I have suffered misfortune; where is the honesty and integrity of nature?"

We bring forward from past existences karma that must be lived out. As we have injured, so must we suffer. Today we are building karma for tomorrow, and if our present life is dedicated to enlightened thinking and living, we are more apt to enjoy the results thereof in a future existence than in this one. However, very often the good deeds of this life have their reward even here. Not only do we bring forward from the past evil karma, but good karma as well; consequently, the average life is a complex of fortune and misfortune, due to the inconsistencies and ignorance of previous lives.

*QUESTION—What is the proper philosophical attitude toward suicide?*

*Answer*—Several newspapers have recently carried accounts of prominent persons who have committed suicide to escape the prolonged inroads of incurable disease. These accounts have raised the question as to the integrity of such action. Is a person justified in ending his own physical life if it appears to be no longer possible for him to live a healthy, normal, and constructive existence?

The attitude of society toward suicide has been subjected to numerous changes and modifications in the thousands of years of social history. Some nations have regarded the action of self-destruction as highly honorable; others have regarded it as commendable under certain extremities; but for the most part, such a course of action has been condemned as irreconcilable with the highest standards of human propriety.

The Mystery Schools of the ancient world were in reasonably complete accord in their condemnation of the deed of suicide. The religio-philosophical institutions taught that self-destruction was an act of violence against the soul. Not that the soul itself could, strictly speaking, be injured, but rather

that suicide was a breach of spiritual ethics. Two examples
will fairly represent the attitude of the ancients.

In the Bacchic and Eleusinian Mysteries, the sacred dramas
exhibited in tableau and pageantry the death of the Universal
Soul deity Dionysus. This god was torn to pieces by the twelve
giants of primordial Chaos who are called the Titans and
represent the irrational elements of the material world. After
these giants had devoured the body of Dionysus, they were
destroyed by the thunderbolt of Zeus who, from their charred
remains, formed as from clay the first human being. The initiates were instructed in the mystical truth that the human
body was composed of a mixture of the elementary substances
and divine essences, the former derived from the ashes of
the Titans, and the latter from the blood of Dionysus or
Bacchus. Any man who raised his hand in violence against
another, or against himself, was guilty of impiety against
the god Dionysus, whose essences were mixed with every part
of the corporeal fabric. Therefore the ancient saying, "Who
strikes himself, strikes the God within him."

Pythagoras held a slightly different view, but the substance
of his opinion agreed in effect with the older teachings of the
original Orphics. According to the Pythagoreans, the physical
body of man was a living temple within the recesses of which
dwelt a divine spirit, one with the eternal nature of God.
The body was therefore a temple sacred to divinity, and to
defile the body was to defame the "secret Master of the house."
This doctrine was so literally enforced that none of the Pythagoreans would permit the body to be mutilated either by
surgery or autopsy, and their opinion so completely dominated
Greek culture that medical science was limited to the clinical
examination of disease.

The Platonic philosophy somewhat modified the rigid views
of the older schools. Suicide was justified in certain ex-

tremities, but the whole subject was circumscribed by profound and exact philosophical rules. For example, an initiate was permitted to take his own life if faced by torture intended to force him to reveal the secrets of the Mysteries. He was also permitted to voluntarily sacrifice his life in the service of his god or in an effort to rescue some unfortunate from extreme danger. He was also permitted this extreme action if it were impossible for him to continue in this life on a level of integrity consistent with the inner development of his own soul. He might choose death before spiritual dishonor.

In no case, however, was suicide permitted in order to escape from sickness, sorrow, responsibility, or any material evil that did not afflict the spirit or render the life incapable of further progress.

Corruption is the inevitable end of all flesh, but the deterioration of material fabric does not justify physical destruction while life, opportunity, and possibilities of philosophical self-improvement remain. A person who discovers that some disease will permit only a few years or even a few months of life should not think first of self-destruction, but rather of the opportunity that yet remains for him to improve in inward knowledge so that he may face the transition with a good hope.

Death is an initiation into the spiritual mysteries of the inner life, and each man should approach the inevitable end fortified with wisdom and vision. Man begins to die the day that he is born, and, as the poet wrote: "The cradle is ever rocking in the open grave." Therefore, everything man accomplishes in this material sphere, he accomplishes while dying. An uninformed man once asked an aged initiate why he did not take his life less strenuously in his declining years. The old sage replied: "Life is a race with time and as my course is nearly run should I cease striving or, like the runner at the games, try harder because the goal is nearer?"

The person contemplating suicide would do well to remember the story told of the Greek philosopher who lay dying in the house of a disciple. The friends were gathered in an outer room when a stranger entered with some gossip of the day. Chancing to look through the doorway into the inner apartment where the philosopher lay dying, they beheld him propped up on one elbow listening attentively to the gossip. One called out to him, "Father, why do you listen to the gossip of this world when you are so soon to leave it?" "I may be dying," the wise man replied, "but I am not yet dead, and while I still live I can still learn."

A wise person does not wreak vengeance upon himself for the evils of his world. He realizes that the purpose of life is the accomplishment of wisdom and experience. Each of the vicissitudes of life brings with it the opportunity to increase knowledge and perfect self. While yet the breath of life is within any body, experience is possible to the soul within that body. Philosophy demands of its disciples that they learn all things well and seek to avoid none of the experiences of this life.

The ancient teaching set forth in symbolic terms the punishments and penalties of suicide. As the great Neoplatonist expressed it: in normal death, the soul separates itself from the body by a natural process. In suicide, the body separates itself from the soul by a violent and irrational action. As this action is contrary to the psychical laws of nature, vibrations are set up which temporarily disrupt the harmony of the soul. For this reason, it is written that the suicide is neither dead nor alive. He has violently destroyed his physical vehicle, but he has not fulfilled the years of his destiny; therefore, he must remain in the superphysical elements of the earth to which his superphysical parts are still attached until the normal span of his life, as set forth in the spiritual archetype of his physical existence, has been completed. To such disembodied, but not decarnated, entities the ancients gave the name of the "undead." They must continue, physical but unseen, until the law of their life has been satisfied.

While this circumstance works no permanent hardship upon the soul, which in its natural time is released from this artificial condition, it works a temporary hardship, and the suicide discovers that his action has delivered him from no evil, released him from no problem, and preserved him from no disaster.

*QUESTION—Please summarize for us a philosophical attitude and policy toward the proper handling and treatment of the bodies of the dead.*

*Answer*—This is a most interesting and practical question, and invites a consideration of several phases of the subject. It seems advisable, therefore, to examine the matter under a number of separate headings.

REASONABLE PREPARATIONS FOR DEATH. Several lawyers of my acquaintance have died intestate. Having helped thousands of clients in the framing of their wills, they have left their own estates in uttter confusion, with the result that their monies and properties have not been distributed as they desired, or have been largely wasted in litigation.

Every thoughtful person should have his estate in order at all times, not because of any morbid fears, but because it is only in this way that the things he has accumulated can fulfill the purposes for which he intended them. In families of moderate means, insurance is now available, by which the burden of a sudden funeral does not descend upon a family already suffering from grief and uncertainty. Procrastination in this matter may work a serious hardship upon surviving members of the family. Philosophy implies thoughtfulness. We should live without injury to others, and when our time comes, die in the same way.

THE SELECTION OF A FUNERAL. It came to my attention recently that a young man, earning fifty dollars a week and supporting a family, burdened himself—under the stress of grief—with a five-thousand-dollar funeral, for which he must pay in monthly installments over a period of five years. While his sentiments were natural and understandable, his action was inconsistent with common sense.

Too many morticians take advantage of the emotional crisis caused by the death of a loved one, and 'sell' funeral arrangements entirely out of proportion with the means of the bereaved family. Usually, the deceased would have resented, could his voice be heard, the wasting of money on the disposition of his remains. If such a contingency is likely to arise, this can often be covered by a frank discussion of the entire subject prior to death.

Personally, I favor the practices of some Oriental peoples who, determining the amount to be spent on a funeral, bury the body as economically as possible and devote the surplus to some memorial project that will advance the causes of the living.

One wealthy New York man requested that at the time of his death, the wide circle of acquaintances that might be expected to deluge his casket with flowers, take the money and bestow it in his name upon an orthopedic hospital that urgently required funds to enlarge its facilities. The letters of acknowledgment for the various gifts were placed on his casket.

Except in the case of public officials whose passing is an important civic event, philosophy dictates modesty in death as in living. Plato requested that his funeral be without ostentation or grief, and that after his body had been placed in its grave, his friends retire to an appropriate place and have a discourse on philosophy in his memory. This was carried out, and the discourse was kept on a serene and pleasant level, the prevailing attitude being that he was still with them.

THE PROPER ATTITUDE TOWARD DEATH. When it is known that the end has come for some loved member of the family, this circumstance requires a wise and gentle behavior of those present at the occasion. The transition should be as peaceful as the nature of the ailment will permit. We should depart from this world as one traveling to a distant land, with the memory of those about us wishing us well and encouraging us on this life's supreme adventure. Though perhaps we have lived in confusion, it is good to die in peace.

Already we are moving on the surface of a strange and secret tide. The physical world is growing dim and distant, and the light of another land is shining upon us through an open door. Our last memories may be the faces of those whom we have known and cherished, or perhaps there are only strangers, or the doctor, or a nurse. In these most holy moments, tears and lamentations, and supplications to remain a little longer, only confuse and sadden the departing guest.

There is a dignity to dying, and many who have not lived well, die well. Those surviving should accept this sacrament of transition with silent and holy understanding, knowing full well that each in his turn must face the end with a good hope.

THE IMMEDIATE TREATMENT OF THE REMAINS. Usually, as soon as the physician announces that death has occurred, the family communicates with a mortician. If death is inevitable, some arrangements should be made in advance, so that it is only necessary to use the telephone. A mortician should be selected who is willing to cooperate with the requirements of the family. It is the prevailing custom to remove the body to the undertaking establishment almost immediately. If this is done reverently and quietly, it is quite proper.

If conditions permit, most students of the esoteric doctrines prefer that a body should not be embalmed until three days after death. In most larger communities, some funeral parlors are equipped with refrigeration facilities. It is advisable to check such facilities well in advance of any probable need. In tropical countries or in small towns, refrigeration may be impossible or much too costly. If such be the case, we should adjust to the existing facilities, just as we adjust to any other emergency that presents itself in life.

It is wrong to assume that the disposition of the body has any permanent or serious effect on the entity after its departure therefrom. There is no reason to regret that we were unable to fulfill such requirements in the past, or to feel that ignorance, neglect, or existing circumstances resulted in any damage to the departed.

The circumstances of death also have an influence in the treatment of the body. Those aged, long ailing, and generally infirm accomplish a complete separation from the body more rapidly than the young person suddenly stricken or killed by accident. Also, ties of responsibility and "unfinished business" have a tendency to hold the entity longer than in cases where the life pattern has been completed.

The final proof of death is the setting-in of the processes of decomposition. The moment these appear, it is no longer necessary to preserve the body. It may then be immediately embalmed, and this is required in many places. Embalming is not detrimental, nor does it cause any inconvenience to the entity after death is complete. Even if the embalming is done before the completion of the three-day period, no damage beyond inconvenience occurs. The three-day period is ideal, but often the ideal must be approximated.

RELIGIOUS SERVICES. It frequently occurs that religious services in connection with the deceased cause conflict and confusion. Where members of a family are of different faiths, it may be difficult to reconcile them, even in the presence of the dead. It has always been my conviction that the primary benefit of a funeral service is the comfort and courage it bestows upon the living. Those who have departed have passed into a spiritual estate beyond the control of man-made sects and creeds. Funeral services, therefore, are an opportunity to express esteem and respect, and should have the simplicity and dignity appropriate to the occasion.

If the deceased did not wish a religious funeral, it seems proper that his desires should be respected, unless these obviously are too great a cause of unhappiness for the survivors. There can be no objections to members of fraternities and societies being buried with the rituals of their Order. Details of the funeral should be determined by good taste and the means available, but should always be modest and moderate.

ULTIMATE DISPOSITION OF THE REMAINS. Many persons designate the disposition they wish for their remains. Where feasible, such instructions should be carried out; where unfeasible, a reasonable compromise may be necessary. One poor family that came under my observation, mortgaged its future and hazarded the security of its children in order to ship the body of a parent half-way around the world to be buried in a family plot. Under such a condition, a family council, with thoughtful consideration of responsibilities to the living, should have arbitrated this sentimental but unreasonable request.

Some indication is usually given during life as to whether the deceased wishes his remains buried or cremated. If there are no strenuous objections, cremation is the most satisfactory means of final disposition. If, however, this is distasteful, burial in the ground or in a mausoleum in no way interferes with the plan of nature. It is unnecessary and unreasonable to pay an exorbitant sum for an elaborate, hermetically sealed casket to preserve the remains for an exaggerated period of time. About the only possible results would be that archeologists, several thousand years from now, might treat the body as scientists of our day have treated the bodies of the Egyptian dead.

MONUMENTS AND MEMORIALS. Imposing structures marking the graves of private citizens are of little interest to strangers or to distant times. Even though the cemetery may promise perpetual care, there seems no good reason why professional caretakers should be entrusted with the maintenance of old memorials. Families convinced that they will make regular pilgrimages to the family shrine seldom return after the first year. Later, the interests of the living take precedence over journeys to the dead. This is quite right, for the world belongs to the living, and they must bear its burden. The simpler way is to sever all outward ties, and depend upon the instincts of the heart to preserve precious remembrances.

It is a serious mistake to preserve in one's personal keeping the ashes of the dead. I know people who have carried these about with them for half a century. It is difficult for such a situation not to end in a generally morbid state of affairs. Some like to scatter the ashes of their loved ones in some garden, from the slopes of a mountain, or upon the surface of the sea. This is acceptable, but more and more difficult to accomplish because of the regulations that have been enacted by groups of morticians.

THE LIVING MUST CARRY ON. The greater tragedy of death is the parting. Those who have gone leave empty places that only the years can fill. We must not prevent, or try to prevent, the healing action of time. Devotion does not mean the perpetuation of sorrow or the impoverishment of our own lives. Although it may sound disloyal, it seems to me that the highest tribute we can pay to those who have gone is to live well without them. If perchance we live better because we have known them, we honor them well.

When loved ones go, they seem to take life with them; but after a little time, if we are deeply thoughtful and of constructive mind, we build life again. Little by little, their once familiar forms retire into the deeper places of our consciousness. New forms take their places. The busy work of the world must be done. We must be faithful to the living and also faithful to our own dreams, which survive all changes of fortune.

We must treat those who precede us through the veil as we in turn wish to be treated. We do not want those whom we love to pine away in grief, or to cloud their years with tears and vain regrets. We like to think that others will carry on our work and fulfill our dreams. We want our sacrifices to bring strength and resolution to those we serve. We want our loved ones to be happy because we have lived, rather than miserable because we have died. Let us then conduct ourselves according to our own convictions of right conduct.

We believe in the immortality of the spirit. We believe in a universe extending through infinite time and infinite space, forever abiding in the wisdom and love of our Eternal Father. We believe that life and death are his laws; and because in his supreme understanding he has fashioned them, we dwell in the faith that they are right.

Against the working of the infinite plan, we raise no voice of objection, no thought of difference. If we know in our hearts the truth of the magnificent plan of which we are part, we will live in the peace of our understanding, accepting all things with gentleness and patience. We truly worship the Creator when we know with such certainty that all difficulties are dissolved, that his ways are good, even though with our minds we do not fully understand.

*QUESTION—Does the doctrine of reincarnation conflict with the teachings of Christianity?*

*Answer*—On at least two occasions, Jesus acknowledged pre-existence, which is almost equivalent to an actual acknowledgment of reincarnation. He certainly referred to his Messianic pre-existence in these words: "Before Abraham was, I am." In another place Jesus declared definitely that his disciples were with him before the beginning of the world. According to the Gospels, these disciples were ordinary men and there is no inference that they should be considered as divine incarnations. To have been with Jesus before the worlds were, implies a vast spiritual existence and a continuity of consciousness over a great extent of time. Jesus also implied that he himself would return to this world, and this Second Coming, toward which so many pious Christians look, would itself establish reincarnation beyond debate. The Master further promised that those who believe in his words shall do greater things even than he has done.

That St. John accepted the doctrine of rebirth is evident from the 12th verse of the 3rd chapter of Revelation: "Him that overcometh will I make a pillar in the temple of my God and *he shall go no more out.*" The words "go no more out" are susceptible of no other interpretation than as a reference to periodic returns to an earthly existence for those who have not yet perfected themselves in the mysteries of life.

To sum up the Biblical situation, there is no definite statement in the Bible concerning reincarnation other than the verse from Revelation just quoted. There are, however, a number of enigmatical statements in which the law of reincarnation seems to be implied. Without this doctrine many of the passages of the Old and New Testaments are meaningless and without point. On the other hand, nowhere in the Jewish or Christian Scriptures is the doctrine of rebirth assailed, denied, criticized, or condemned. The whole subject, therefore, is not a doctrinal issue, and the belief in reincarnation cannot be dismissed as heretical from the words of Jesus or the prophets.

The prevalence of the belief in reincarnation in the first centuries of the Christian era is evidenced by its wide acceptance by the early Greek and Latin fathers of the Christian Church. It appears also that the Essenes, a religious order of which Jesus is supposed to have been a member, accepted the doctrine of rebirth, having derived knowledge of it from Pythagoras, the founder of their order. The Gnostics, the most learned of Christian orders, and the first heretics, taught reincarnation and claimed to have derived their mystical traditions from a disciple of St. Matthew. Reincarnation was defended by many fathers of the early Church, among them Origen, Justin Martyr, Clemens Alexandrinus, Nemesius, Synesius, Hilarius, and Arnobius. Probably the most outspoken of these Christian patriarchs was Origen, a man who combined a high degree of philosophical insight and true Christian piety. He writes of reincarnation in this fashion:

"Is it not more in conformity with reason that every Soul for certain mysterious reasons (I speak now according to the opinions of Pythagoras, Plato and Empedocles whom Celsus frequently names) is introduced into a body, and introduced according to *its deserts and former actions?*"

It is generally believed that in the sixth century A.D. the Fifth Council of Constantinople anathematized reincarnation, but it is now evident that this prevailing prejudice is unfounded. To quote the Rev. A. Henderson, Vicar of St. John de Sepulchre, Norwich:

"A further objection which exists in the minds of many is based on the supposed condemnation of the doctrine by the Church in the Fifth General Council of Constantinople. A careful consideration of the historical situation makes it abundantly clear that the question of reincarnation was not even raised at the Council and that the condemnation of certain extreme tenets of the Origenists was the act of Mennas, Patriarch of Constantinople, in the Provincial Synod. In this he was instigated by the Emperor Justinian who ordered him to procure the subscription of the bishops to the anathemas. This local synod was held in A. D. 543, while the General Council did not meet until ten years later. It is easy to understand, however, how this extra-conciliar sentence of Mennas was, at a later period, mistaken for a decree of the General Council."

The above quotation clarifies two points of controversy: first, the problem of reincarnation was not even considered by the Fifth General Council; second, the Provincial Synod directed against the Origenists makes no specific reference to reincarnation, and there is no way of proving that the doctrine of rebirth was even one of the "extreme tenets" which had irritated Justinian. It therefore follows, as Mr. G. R. S. Mead, an eminent scholar in matters of early Christian tradition, has observed, that the Christian Church has never formally anathematized reincarnation.

E. D. Walker, in his valuable work *Reincarnation,* includes the illustrious name of St. Buenaventura among the many churchmen who favored the doctrine. Prof. Wincenty Luto-slawski, in his important book *Pre-existence and Reincarnation,* writes thus of rebirth:

"It finds favor even with Roman Catholic theologians, amongst whom was the great scholar, Monsignor Archbishop Passavalli (1820-1897) who not only declared that reincarnation is not in conflict with Catholic dogma, but himself accepted the doctrine, at the age of sixty-two, from two disciples of the Polish School of Philosophy, and 'lived up to the age of seventy-two, unshaken in his conviction that he had lived many times on earth and that he was likely to return'."

The attitude of the Christian Church in the twentieth century on the vital issue of reincarnation is best summarized in the opinions of two leading churchmen. Cardinal Mercier, the heroic Prelate of the Belgians, representing the opinions of the Roman Catholic faith, while not committing himself to a personal belief in reincarnation, has definitely stated that the doctrine is not in conflict with Catholic dogma. For

Protestant Christianity, Dean Inge, late of St. Paul's in London, assumes a similar attitude, finding no conflict between this "the oldest creed" and modern Episcopalianism.

From the preceding, there is reasonable assurance that the modern Christian can incorporate the doctrine of reincarnation as a part of his religious belief and remain safe within "the odour of sanctity."

# THE MYSTERY SCHOOLS

## PART FIVE

*QUESTION—What is meant by the Ancient Wisdom and the "Mysteries?"*

*Answer*—The *Ancient Wisdom* is the body of occult knowledge that has descended from the remote beginning of civilization to the present time. According to the traditions of antiquity, certain divinely inspired teachers, graduates of earlier life cycles, incarnated during the Lemurian and early Atlantean periods, bringing to the present human race the foundations of spiritual, philosophical, and scientific knowledge. Occult philosophy teaches that the Ancient Wisdom was entrusted to the keeping of certain of the most highly evolved priests of the ancient world. These priests, as custodians of the secrets of life, set about to accomplish the gradual education of the human race. The average man, then as now, was unable to receive the more profound aspects of knowledge. Therefore, simpler doctrines were devised to meet the needs of the unenlightened, and the more profound truths were reserved for the advanced types of humanity.

The *Mysteries,* or colleges of the Ancient Wisdom, were schools of preparation in which men and women were trained in the science of living, and received the preparation necessary for enlightenment. The Mystery Schools were therefore the guardians of the Ancient Wisdom, and were, for the most part, founded by initiate-priest-philosophers who had received

119

the esoteric wisdom from the demigods of the first ages. In the Mysteries candidates were tested as to their strength of character, their courage, their integrity, and their intelligence. The initiations, given in the old Mystery Schools, were trials of spiritual, mental, and physical strength. Those who passed the initiations satisfactorily were accepted into the body of the priesthood and were instructed in the secrets of the Ancient Wisdom.

Briefly stated, the Ancient Wisdom is eternal Truth, and the Mysteries are the physical institution by which man's consciousness is refined until he is capable of participating in divine Truth.

*QUESTION—Name the principal schools of the ancient Mysteries.*

*Answer*—Schools of initiation into the Mysteries of the Ancient Wisdom flourished among most of the civilizations of antiquity. We most commonly think of the Mysteries in connection with the cultural systems of Greece and Egypt. The principal Mysteries celebrated among the Greeks were the Eleusinian, Dionysian, Sabazian, Samothracian, and Cretan. In addition to these state institutions, there were associations of philosophers whose schools should be properly included among the Mysteries. The most important of such groups were the Pythagorean and Platonic schools. Some of the Grecian Mysteries were carried to Rome and flourished under the Caesars.

The principal Mysteries of the Chaldeans were the rites of Ishtar and Tammuz, and the cult of Izdubar. The Persian Mysteries were called Magian, and were founded upon the teachings of Zoroaster. The Mithraic cult arose from the

Magian rites. It was celebrated in Rome, and was carried by the Roman Legions to France and England. The Druidic Mysteries were celebrated in both Britain and Gaul, and combined doctrines from both Chaldean and Buddhistic sources. The Odinic or Gothic rites were peculiar to the Scandinavian and Germanic countries, and were founded by Prince Sigge, commonly known as Odin, who migrated from the Mesopotamian area.

The principal Mystery cults of the Egyptians were the rites of Isis, Osiris, and Horus. The various cities of ancient Egypt had their own tutelary gods, and the Mysteries of these gods were celebrated in their own communities. The rites of Serapis appeared in Egypt during the period of the Ptolemies, and flourished until the fourth century A. D.

In Syria, the most important school was the Essene, and somewhat similar in nature were the Nazarenes and Therapeutae. Several mystical sects rose among the Jews after the Mosaic Mysteries. Possibly the most significant was the Cabalistic school, which had its beginning during the Roman conquest of Judea. Christianity was celebrated as a Mystery School during the first three centuries of the faith; and among Christian mystical organizations should be included the Gnostics and the followers of Marcion.

Institutions of initiation rose among the Arabs under the patronage of Islam. The Dervishes and the Sufis are the most important of these societies. The Yezidee of Iraq, of dubious reputation, was a secret society with a stronghold at Mount Alamont. The Druses are a secret society still surviving in the Near East.

Buddhist Mysteries were performed in the Septaparna caverns by the early Arhats; and important Brahmanical initiation existed at Ellora and Elephanta.

The Mysteries are still celebrated in Tibet and Mongolia under the general title of Lamaism. China has its Taoist doctrines in which the initiations are mostly institutes of self-discipline. Shinto and Buddhist rites are celebrated in Japan, and contain the same elements present in the classical schools.

Several schools of initiation existed in ancient America. State Mysteries flourished among the Inca, Maya, Aztec and North American tribes. The Midewiwin, or great Medicine Lodge of the Ojibway, is an example of a North American Mystery School. The rites of Xibalba, practiced in Guatemala, are a type of the Central American Mysteries. Shamanism exercised a powerful force in Siberia, and the Alaskan Indians and Eskimos derived their Mysteries from the nomads of Asia.

In fact we may say that no nation and no age has been without its esoteric schools. Of more modern origin are the Illuminati, Rosicrucians, Alchemists and Freemasons. These orders all appeared in the 16th and 17th centuries, but unfortunately have fallen away from their esoteric traditions. Their teachings are now practiced by sincere individuals who derive their doctrines from the early books and manuscripts of these orders.

*QUESTION—What is the Great White Lodge?*

*Answer*—For thousands of years, Oriental peoples have united in venerating a mysterious order of adepts or initiates who gather at regular intervals to hold secret conclave on the high plateaus of Trans-Himalaya. It is believed by the best informed students of the occult philosophies that the great initiates of the world together constitute a governing body of super-human beings, vastly superior to ordinary mortals in wisdom and understanding. This council of adepts is generally referred to as the Great White Lodge, or invisible government of the earth.

For nearly a hundred years, the British government in India has been trying to undermine the Hindu's faith in Mahatmas and Arhats, but today that faith remains strong and vital, and the length and breadth of Hindustan is bound together by a common faith in the existence of immortal mortals. The Chinese still speak of their Sages of the Snowy Mountains who come down from caves, and, crossing the great deserts, are seen entering and leaving through the Northern portals of the Great Wall. These sages are titled in the Chinese language the Sublime Ageless Ones from the Great White Mountain. Even the overthrow of the Manchus and the antireligious influence of communism in China have not shaken the faith of the people in supernatural sages.

Curiously enough, these magician-philosophers have been partly incorporated into the hero worship of the Chinese and appear, thinly veiled, in the worship of the Joss or interceding heroes. The worship of Mahatmas in China is closely associated with Buddhism, and the mysterious sages are usually believed to be masters of either Hindu or Tibetan Mahayana Buddhism.

Among the Egyptians, the great mountain of the world, the Meru or Shamballah, was represented by a mound, a dome-shaped hieroglyphic, surmounted by the axe or symbol or sign of the gods, sometimes called a banner. There is a tradition that the term Great White Lodge was derived from the supreme council or college of the priests of the nomes of Egypt. This council met at Memphis, the city of the white walls, or as it is sometimes referred to, the great white city. The Egyptians were well informed in the secret doctrines of Asia and, like most ancient peoples, acknowledged the "Secret

Power of the North," a name for the Trans-Himalayan adepts. The council of Memphis was unquestionably a branch of the Great School.

Unfortunately, many misconceptions have arisen in the West as to the nature and function of the Great White Lodge. Not only has its purpose been misunderstood, but the very names of the teachers or masters who compose it have been subjected to profanation. In the last years, pseudo-occult organizations have arisen actually claiming either to be the Great White Lodge or to represent it. Needless to say, the great school of Asia does not flourish as a corporate body, nor does it advertise for members in cheap magazines. Certainly it does not offer membership, correspondence courses, diplomas, or free literature. As far as the average student of metaphysics is concerned, the Great White Lodge is merely a name signifying the deepest and most mysterious force at work in the world, a force entirely too venerable, too sacred, to be associated with the commercial and physical issues of knowledge.

Knowledge of the existence of the Great White Lodge came to the West principally through the writings of Madame H. P. Blavatsky and her teachers the Mahatmas M. and K. H. These writings are the fountainhead of Western occultism, and many schools have sprung up giving interpretations or misinterpretations of Madame Blavatsky's work. In the closing years of the 19th century, America and Europe became definitely conscious of occult lore. The Mysteries of Asia flowed into Western minds, to color the thought and culture of the Occident. Now, after the lapse of some fifty years, we realize that the West has neither the background nor the spiritual sensitivity to sense or appreciate the religious mysticism of Asia. Unable to understand the Mahatmas or to grasp the significance of the Great School, bound hopelessly to the literal and the evident, and untrained in subtleties, the West has missed the vision. The metaphysical foundations of the 19th century have led to a hopeless chaos in the 20th century. Mediumship has been mistaken for mastery, psychism and charlatanism have perverted and obscured the whole issue, until it is extremely difficult for sincere students to find any sure and certain course of procedure.

The Great White Lodge is the hierarchy of enlightened souls bound together by wisdom and dedicated to the service of human need. Its lowest parts are composed of lay students and truth seekers whose virtue is sincerity. It ascends to the various degrees of studentship, probationship, and discipleship until the degree of adept or arhat is reached. The degrees still ascend through the various levels of initiates, until the whole order has as its apex and head the secret Nameless and Unknown One, whom the Egyptians called the Master of the Secret House. In the definition of the Hindu, the Great White Lodge is the hands and feet of the Lord of the World. It is the peculiar body of Truth, and its members together constitute a composite organism through which the Formless Wisdom is interpreted and manifested.

The Trans-Himalayan area of Shamo or Gobi Desert, formed in prehistoric times the Sacred Island and the great sea in the midst of which rose a strange out-cropping of Azoic rock. This out-cropping is referred to as the Imperishable Land. According to the ancient traditions, it was the first area of solid substance to appear in the process of the earth's cooling. This area was the North Pole, where the motion of rotation was the slowest. According to the Tibetans, it was upon this North Polar cap, called the Lotus Crown of the Earth Mother, that the gods descended in the first day. According to the same tradition, all the races of man have had their beginnings on the shores of Gobi, the ocean of sand,

and from the high Himalaya country have spread about the earth. All races also in the end return to Gobi to die, and the altar of the First Man is said to stand on the out-cropping of Azoic rock at the edge of Gobi. For this reason, the Imperishable Island is the most sacred place on earth, and it is here that the house of the everlasting faith stands, for Gobi is not only the birth-place of the races and the homeland of all living things; it is the seed-ground of the faiths of the world. To the Asiatic mind, life and faith are one, and the streams of wisdom flow forth from the fountains of life. As the races are many, though their source is One, so the faiths of man are many but their source is what Mohammed called the Primordial Faith—the one Truth that all faiths share in part.

QUESTION—*In what way does an Initiate or Adept differ from an ordinary person?*

*Answer*—First we must define our terms. Although the words are often used interchangeably, *initiate* and *adept* have different meanings. Technically, an initiate is any person who has been accepted into a body of secret knowledge by some special ritual or ceremony. In ancient times, the term *initiate* signified a man or woman who had passed through the ordeals of the state Mysteries or religio-philosophical institutions of spiritual education. In modern occultism, an initiate is a person who has been accepted into one of the secret schools of natural occultism. In this sense of the word, initiation follows years of probationship and preparation. All true initiation is an inner mystical experience and should never be confused with the ritualism of any physical institution, no matter how metaphysical the ritual itself may be in its implications.

The word *adept* signifies one who is proficient in the use of the occult forces of nature, and many years or even lives are required after initiation before this proficiency is acquired. In antiquity, the term *adept* was reserved for those who had received the Great Mysteries. They were a small group within the body of the initiates themselves. An adept is one proficient in the most highly advanced sciences of the Mystery School. There are many initiates to one adept.

It should be distinctly remembered that both initiates and adepts are human beings, part of our own life wave, differing from ordinary mortals only in the unfoldment of their subjective spiritual nature. The initiate is wiser than the average person, and the adept is wiser than the initiate. Yet this wisdom should not be regarded as superhuman, but rather as a type of enlightened condition toward which the whole race is being moved by the law of evolution. An initiate is subject to the same laws that govern the average man. He is born, he must eat and sleep, and he will pass out of his body in the same way that others do. He is simply equipped to live more constructively and more usefully because he possesses a truer vision of the workings of universal law. The initiate is usually clairvoyant to some degree, as this is necessary to his initiation. He may or may not possess the ability to function consciously outside of the physical body. He can read part of the etheric record of the earth, and has a considerable understanding of the invisible worlds. He is able to commune with others of a similar degree of development by subjective methods, and he is part of that great Brotherhood of initiates which is being built up in the world as the foundation for the philosophical era that is to come.

All that we have here noted is also true of the adept, but his powers are considerably amplified. He has become part of the mechanism of the Great School itself, and unlike the initiate, he is not apt to mingle commonly in society, but will live apart in some center of the brethren. If he appears among men, it is incognito, except to other members of his Order. He is a conscious instrument of the Great Plan and perpetuates his body without the phenomena of birth and death. He does not have disciples other than initiates, and it is exceedingly unlikely that he will make his appearance to any person not already highly proficient in occult matters. There is no way in which the average layman can detect an initiate or an adept. But those who have developed a spiritual sensitivity can feel the vibrations of these advanced people. There are also peculiarities in the aura by which they can be detected by those capable of perceiving these superphysical emanations from the body.

It should particularly be borne in mind that the state of initiation or adeptship does not release man from the laws governing human life; nor will any adept of the White Path ever break natural laws or encourage others to do so. No initiate or adept will use occult power to avoid physical responsibility or pain. It is a law of the Schools that the supernatural powers which man develops must never be used personally or selfishly. It is said of the adept of Galilee: "Others he could help, but himself he could not save."


*QUESTION—The expectation of the coming of a World Teacher seems to be widespread, being as common in Asia as in this country. Is there a justification for this expectation?*

*Answer*—Among the better informed students of the esoteric traditions, there is no immediate expectation of the advent of a World Teacher. This does not mean that heroic personalities will not appear to aid the progress of the race. There is seldom a time when emissaries of the Great School are not at work in the world. The fifth race, our race, has already received its spiritual revelation, and no other major revelation can be expected until we have applied the wisdom that has already been given to us. About the year 1975 the next emissary of the Great White Lodge is expected. This representative will not be regarded as a World Teacher, but merely as one of a long line of instructors who appear in the closing quarter of each century. The Lord Maitreya, whose coming is awaited in Asia, and who, in terms of Tibetan metaphysics, has already "lowered one foot from his throne of the golden lotus," will be the World Teacher of the sixth root race, and his coming cannot be expected until the nucleus of the sixth root race is fairly well integrated. In the meantime, disciples of the ancient wisdom receive their instruction from the "ever-coming Lord" within themselves.


QUESTION—*What is black magic?*

*Answer*—Black magic is the perversion or misuse of the occult forces of nature. This misuse may arise either from ignorance or from a premeditated and intentional misapplication of spiritual powers. All universal forces are universal in their purposes. Proficiency in the occult arts brings with it a certain ability to influence and direct the subtle elements of the universe. The white magician uses his knowledge for the good of all, and the black magician uses his for the benefit of himself, usually at the expense of others.

All black magic has its origin in selfishness or egotism. The forces used by the black magician are identical with those in white magic. It is the motive and not the action itself which determines right and wrong use of occult powers. The individual who attempts to use spiritual means to accomplish material ends is playing with fire. Sorcery is an ever-present temptation in the life of the metaphysician. Only a solid groundwork in ethics and integrity can prevent disaster.

Vice, like virtue, has its beginning in small matters. A considerable part of what is now called popular metaphysics is dabbling with black magic. People who are always "holding the thought" for some kind of prosperity, or are trying to influence the lives of others by various systems of mental suggestion, are starting careers of black magic that may lead to unsuspected tragedy. Any individual who tries, by any method of the occult sciences, to escape responsibility for action or gain that which is not earned by his own effort, has his foot on the slippery path of the black magician.

According to the old traditions, the perverted priests of Atlantis built temples to demons and arrayed the forces of darkness against the hierophants of the true religion. From that time to the present day, perverted adepts have founded perverted orders and have preyed like werewolves upon the unwary. Nearly all the great religions of the world have been attacked by renegade cults that have sprung up in their midst. The path of absolute integrity is a difficult one, and a certain class of society has always been willing, like Faust, to barter the immortal soul in exchange for temporal powers and privileges. Any achievement gained at the expense of others brings with it a proportionately heavy karma. The lot of the tyrant may seem attractive here, but in the larger world, those who live by the sword perish by it also.

In the writings of ancient India, it is recorded that the temple of the gods upon the earth was the polar city of Shamballah. The northern hemisphere was the dwelling place of the Suryas, the spirits of light. When the gods had fashioned their house in the north, the powers of evil built theirs in the south. The temple of the dark forces is described as being in the gloom of the South Pole; and here gathered the Asuryas, the spirits that were against the light. Thus began the warfare of light and darkness, of spirit and matter, of wisdom and ignorance, of virtue and vice, of the spirit and the body. The conflicts in the inner life must continue until the powers of evil are overcome; until Lucifer, the personal self, is routed from the heavens and with his legion of evil spirits, the destructive thoughts and emotions, hurled into the abyss.

Certain metaphysicians are afflicted with the type of reasoning accredited to a Zulu priest. This worthy medicine doctor explained to a missionary that his people made no offerings to God, because he was good and would not hurt them; it was therefore far more propitious to please the spirit of evil, who might bring a famine or a plague upon them at a moment's notice.

Black magic is a phobia among occult students. Everything that goes wrong is attributed to the forces of evil when, in the majority of cases, it is only the result of the individual's stupidity. Black magicians are not the causes of ordinary metaphysical problems. We have contacted many people who believed that the whole force of hell was conspiring to drag them to perdition when, in reality, they were suffering from a highly overstrained imagination. Metaphysical students should remember that black magic is powerless unless the individual himself compromises his own standard of right and wrong.

The schools of black magic are the negative shadows of the schools of white magic. Every school of white magic has a certain doctrine. In every case, this doctrine can be perverted, and its perversion constitutes black magic. Most of the black schools have no names, but are the left-hand paths of the white schools. As white magic may be Christian, Buddhist, Brahman, Jewish or Chinese, so the schools of black magic bear the same distinguishing titles. But it was the habit in the Mysteries to represent the black school by reversing or inverting the name of the white school.

The sorceresses of Thessaly, the Black Hat Lamas of Tibet, the witchcraft and lycanthropy of Europe, and African Voodoo, are examples of cults dominated by black forces. Sects of black magicians exist today on all the continents. In Europe and America their sphere of influence is limited to a degenerate class of society or to people who have not the common sense to recognize evident degeneracy, when it is thinly cloaked with religious ceremonial.

Black forces may be accepted as powerful factors in any period of cultural degeneracy, but it should be remembered that evil can work only through an appropriate medium. War, crime, degeneracy, and perversion release the dark forces upon society; and the battle of darkness and light must go on through the ages until wisdom and virtue perfect in man a permanent standard of integrity.

QUESTION—*In what way does Rosicrucianism differ from other wisdom religions and when did it have its beginning?*

Answer—Rosicrucianism as it is now popularly taught is an interpretation of the old Mystery teachings in the light of Christianity. It therefore differs from all pre-Christian movements, and from the occult schools of non-Christian peoples, principally in its interpretation of the significance of Christ. To the ancient pagans and to the non-Christians of the modern world, Christ is either a Universal Principle independent of time and place, or the Messianic attributes are bestowed also upon the prophets or leaders of these other faiths.

Like nearly all metaphysical movements, Rosicrucian history is obscure, and where facts are few, fables are never wanting. Modern writers upon the subject of the Rosicrucians have fallen into extravagant statements concerning the antiquity of the Order. These statements are for the most part founded upon the highly allegorical account of the antiquity of the Rosicrucian masters, published by John Heydon in the last half of the 17th century. History, however, fails to justify Heydon's flights, and his fantastic story can never be accepted as literally true, although, symbolically speaking, it contains much of vital interest.

The Rosicrucianism of the 17th century was a philosophical rather than a religious movement. Its members were Cabalists, Alchemists, Hermetists, astrologers, and disciples of the transcendental arts, but when called upon to make a declaration of their faith, the members of the original Society acknowledged allegiance to the Lutheran Church in Germany or the Reformed Church of England. The Rosicrucian Society is popularly supposed to have been founded about the year 1610 by a German Lutheran theologian, Johann Valentin Andreae. Our researches incline us to believe that the Society was actually founded about 1604, probably by Lord Bacon, and was composed of such disciples and initiates of the old Hermetic Mysteries as had survived the Inquisition in Europe.

No bona fide records of the Rosicrucian Society have been discovered that can be dated earlier than the year 1600. In fact, prior to 1610 little of tangible definition has been discovered. The Society itself most certainly came into actual existence about the beginning of the 17th century. Its first publication may have been circulated in manuscript between 1600 and 1610, but the earliest published evidence of the Order did not appear until 1612, when several editions of the *Fame and Confession of the Rose Cross* were in circulation.

It is our opinion, based on considerable examination, that Rosicrucianism, like Christianity, was not a spontaneous revelation but an outgrowth of a chain of adequate causes. Mystical societies in Europe can be traced back through the Dark Ages and finally mingle themselves with the pagan Mysteries of the early centuries of the Christian era. If we speak of Rosicrucianism as a mystical tradition, we can trace it back to Egypt and Atlantis, but when we speak of it as a Society of men functioning under the laws and regulations of a physical society, organized under the name Rosicrucianism, we must then limit ourselves to the opening years of the 17th century.

From about 1610 down to the closing years of the 18th century, the history of the Rosicrucians is rather well established. We have the names and titles of most of the officers of the Order, and a fairly complete account of their rituals and grades and the various reorganizations through which the Society passed.

By the beginning of the 19th century, the legitimate history is obscured by so involved a complex of spurious accounts that we may say that the history of the Society vanishes in a general confusion.

After describing the purposes of their organization, the Rosicrucians in their first manifestos recount the adventures of their leader and how he came to establish the Society. The story is briefly as follows:

Father C. R. C. (Christian Rosenkreutz, or Rose Cross) was the son of poor but noble parents, and was placed in a cloister when but five years of age. Several years later, finding the instruction unsatisfactory, he associated himself with a monk who was about to start on a pilgrimage for the Holy Land. This brother died at Cyprus, and C. R. C. continued alone to Damascus. Here poor health detained him, and he remained for some time, studying with the physicians and astrologers. Hearing by chance of a group of wise men abiding in Damcar, a mysterious city in Arabia, C. R. C. made arrangements to visit them, and arrived in Damcar in the sixteenth year of his life. He was received by the wise men as one long expected, and remained with them for a considerable time, during which he learned the Arabian tongue and translated the mysterious book "M" into Latin. From Damcar he journeyed to Fez, where he was instructed concerning the creatures existing in the elements. From Fez the young initiate took ship to Spain, carrying with him many rare medicines, curious animals, and wonderful books. He conferred with the learned at Madrid, but they dared not accept his teachings because this would reveal their previous ignorance. So, deeply discouraged, he went to Germany, where he built himself a house on the brow of a little hill and devoted his life to study and experimentation.

After a silence of five years, C. R. C. gathered about him a few faithful friends, and they began to arrange and classify the great knowledge he possessed. Thus, the Rosicrucian Fraternity was founded. New members were later accepted, and the brethren traveled into various parts of the world to give their knowledge to those who were worthy and willing to receive such a boon. The first of the Order to die passed on in England, and it was after this that Father C. R. C. prepared his own tomb, a perfect miniature reproduction of the universe. None of the Order knew when their founder passed on, but 120 years after his death they discovered his tomb with an ever-burning lamp suspended from the ceiling. The room had seven sides, and in the center of it was a circular stone under which they found the body of their founder in perfect condition, clasping in one hand a mysterious paper containing the Arcana of the Order.

Many efforts have been made to interpret the symbolism of this allegory, for it is undoubtedly a myth, symbolically setting forth the deepest secrets of the Rosicrucians. Father C. R. C. is to be considered not only as a personality, but also as the personification of a power or principle in nature. This practice of using an individual to set forth the workings of divine power was frequently resorted to by the ancients. The Masonic legend of Hiram Abiff, the Chaldean myth of Ishtar, the Greek allegory of Bacchus, and the Egyptian account of Osiris are all examples of this type of symbolism. It is not improbable that the entire mystery of Rosicrucianism could be cleared up if the story of Father C. R. C. were properly interpreted.

During the 16th century, many pseudo organizations sprang up claiming to represent the Rosicrucian Brotherhood, but the very nature of the teachings they promulgated proved beyond all doubt that they were fraudulent. One of these groups, after exacting the most terrible oaths from those joining the society, gave each of the new members a black rope with which he was supposed to strangle himself if he broke any of the laws of the order. The pseudo-Rosicrucians were short-lived, for after passing through all the degrees of the elaborate rituals and spending considerable sums of money, the unfortunate "initiates" discovered that these organizations did not possess the knowledge they claimed to disseminate.

Many false claims were made by charlatans who attempted to capitalize on the name Rosicrucian, but in some mysterious way, these dishonest parties were exposed and their plans came to naught.

The bona fide Rosicrucians are an organization of initiates and adepts, and only through development of the internal spiritual faculties can the true purpose of the Order be recognized. Only when the disciple lives the Rosicrucian life can he know that sublime fraternity whose members—the old books declare—inhabit the suburbs of heaven.


*QUESTION—What is the Cabala?*

*Answer*—The Cabala has been called the Secret Doctrine of Israel, and is one of the most important sources of the ancient wisdom teachings. Eliphas Levi, the French Cabalist, wrote that the three most important books of the Cabala are the *Zohar,* the *Sepher Yetzirah,* and the *Apocalypse.* The *Zohar* has been recently translated into English for the first time. The *Sepher Yetzirah* can be ordered from any bookstore dealing in second-hand occult books. Several editions exist in English. In addition to these works, there are several authors who have explained or interpreted Cabalistic thought. Isaac Myer, Arthur Edward Waite, Franck, Ginsburg and MacGregor have written readable works on the subject. The great textbook of Cabalism is the *Kabbala Denudata,* published in 1677, in Latin only, by Knorr von Rosenroth. This book may be consulted in the San Francisco public library, the New York City public library, in the Library of Congress, and in our own collection.

Books dealing with the numerology of the Cabala are extremely scarce. The only works I have on the subject are in manuscript. Authentic books on any phase of numerology are extremely rare, and the popular available writings are of doubtful importance. Stanley's *History of Philosophy* has a good article on the Pythagorean theory of numbers. Thomas Taylor's *Theoretic Arithmetic* is the most important textbook available on this subject. Wynn Westcott's *Numbers* is a small but interesting handbook. I hope at some future time to be able to publish some of the old manuscripts on numerology in our collection.

Cabalism, as a method for interpreting the metaphysics of the Old Testament, had its origin among the Jews at about the beginning of the Christian era. Tradition bestows great antiquity upon Cabalistic speculations. There is said to have been a school of the angels before the Fall of Man. The angel Raziel taught the secrets of the Cabala to Adam in the Garden of Eden. Noah, Abraham, Moses, David and Solomon are said to have been masters of Cabalistic philosophy.

Rabbi Akiba was the author of the *Sepher Yetzirah,* or the Book of the Formations, and critical scholars date the Cabalistic school from his time, A. D. 120. The *Sepher Ha Zohar* was written about A. D. 170, but remained practically unknown until the 14th Century of the Christian era. The first of these describes the creation of the universe according to a system of emanations based upon the letters of the Hebrew alphabet. The second book is an elaborate work on cosmogony, anthropology and psychology, interpreting the secrets of the Bible according to a system involving magic, astrology, numerology and Hermeticism.

Briefly stated, Cabalism describes the universe as consisting of four great emanations out of Ain Soph, the boundless absolute First Principle. The world is a great symbolical tree, with its roots in heaven and its branches on the earth. All life is part of One Life which, flowing through all things, animates and sustains them. The theory of the Macrocosm and the Microcosm is clearly set forth. The world is a great man, and man is a little world. Man discovers the universe by understanding himself, and the law of analogy is a bridge in space uniting the lesser and the greater.

Transcendental and talismanic magic is strongly involved; also necromancy. Deriving authority from the *Key of Solomon,* a work on spirits attributed to the King of Israel, the Cabalists bound the angels, chained the demons, and made pacts for various purposes with the invisible forces of nature. It is the necromancy and sorcery of the Cabala that has caused this great science to fall into disrepute among orthodox Jews. While the ceremonial magic of the Cabala offers little but hazard, the philosophical aspects of the doctrine are of the greatest significance to all students of the occult sciences.

*QUESTION—What is Gnostic Christianity and does it contain the esoteric teachings of Christ?*

*Answer*—Gnosticism was the great heresy of the ante-Nicene period of church history. The fathers of incipient Christianity, having elected themselves the custodians of salvation, exercised this prerogative to stamp out all traces of Christianity as a philosophical code. By exiling reason from the gatherings of the elect and substituting blind faith in its stead, they accomplished what they considered the first and most necessary step toward the establishment of dogmatic ecclesiasticism.

The Gnostics occupied an extremely precarious position. They were reconcilers of doctrines; and the way of the peacemaker is usually quite as hard as that of the transgressor. Gnosticism was despised by the Church because it sought to interpret Christian mysticism in terms of the metaphysical systems of the Greeks, Egyptians, and Chaldeans. At the same time, it was openly opposed by contemporary pagan philosophers—particularly certain of the Neo-Platonists—because it appeared to accent, at least in part, the unphilosophic and illogical tenets forced upon the world by the Christian enthusiasts. Attacked from both sides, and gradually crushed by the sheer weight of numbers, after a desperate struggle for existence over a period of several centuries, Gnosticism finally passed into limbo. Though the Gnostics have vanished from the earth, the analogies between Christian and pagan doctrines established by them have proved invaluable to students of comparative religion fortunate enough to be born in a less intolerant age.

Among the names that stand out in the chronicles of Gnosticism three are pre-eminent—Simon Magus, Basilides, and Valentinus. That they were men of exceptional brilliance is established by the fact that the attacks of the church fathers were in nearly every case directed first against them. The only fragments of the writings of these great Gnostics are preserved in the writings of their enemies, but such writings reveal not only a high degree of spiritual insight, but a most generous, noble, and philosophic comprehension of the greater realities of life. Even the calumny of the ages has not dimmed the splendor of these masters, nor hidden their glory from such as have eyes to see. If the true secrets of Christianity were ever imparted to men, it was to the Gnostics; for while the Church itself was a seething mass of bigotry and conspiracy, this order preserved to the end the high ethical and rational standards that confer honor upon every sublime teaching.

The church fathers considered the period of Gnosticism to be the most crucial in the history of Christianity, for at that time it had to be decided whether the new cult should be a *religion* or a *philosophy*. If the Gnostics had won, Christianity would have been regarded as the legitimate heir to the philosophic wisdom of preceding ages and would have gone forward as an interpretation of all the great systems and teachers that had preceded it. When the Church succeeded in dominating the situation, it was decreed that the new revelation should become a *faith* and retain its isolated infallibility so that its hand was against every unbeliever. To the Gnostics, Christianity was a *key;* to the Christians it was a sect.

The Gnostic interpretation was premature. The world desired to worship rather than to think, to pray rather than to work. Christ as a personal god, as preached by Peter, was understandable by the mob; but Christ as a Universal Principle, as originally revealed by St. Paul, was incomprehensible. Christianity became a lazy man's faith, and from its peculiar psychology were created those modern attitudes which are now threatening to ruin a civilization. It became a competitive doctrine and a religion of special privileges.

In summing up the doctrine of Gnosticism, we may say that from a simple cult it evolved into an elaborate system, uniting within itself the essential factors of several great faiths. The central idea of Gnosticism is the ascent of the soul through successive stages of being, a series of heavens, each under the rule of a planetary god. Through these the soul must make its ascent by means of magical passwords delivered to the guardians of the doors. (See the *Encyclopedia of Religion and Ethics.*)

This ladder of the worlds, upon which souls ascend and descend, is described in the Babylonian myth of Tammuz and

Ishtar. It appears also in the *Divine Pymander* of Hermes, where seven planetary governors sit upon the seven concentric circles of the world through which souls ascend and descend. The symbolism appears once more in the Royal Arches of Enoch, and in the Revelation of St. John. The commentaries upon Mohammed's Night Journey to Heaven describe how the Prophet, after climbing a ladder of golden cords, passed through seven gates, at each of which stood one of the patriarchs to receive his word and to beseech him to intercede for them at the divine footstool.

There is much in Gnosticism to intrigue the Orientalist. Bardesanes, the last of the Gnostics, admitted himself to have been influenced by East Indian (Buddhist) metaphysics. This is particularly evident in that part of the cult in which Christ is described as descending through the seven worlds on his way to physical incarnation. Like the Buddha, he ensouls a body on each of these planes, thus literally becoming all things unto all men. Like the Oriental thought, also, is the ultimate condition to which Gnosticism aspires. The soul is finally absorbed into an abstract state perfectly analagous to Nirvana, so that the end of existence is the condition of not-being.

In the simplest arrangement of the Gnostic Godhead, we find first the Universal Logos—he who stood, stands, and will stand. By nature and substance unknowable, he is the incorruptible form who projects from himself an image, and this image ordains all things. From its own eternal and imperishable nature That Which Abides emits three hypostases, which Simon Magus calls *Incorruptible Form,* the *Great Thought,* and the *Universal Mind.* Among the later Gnostics, the Godhead is represented thus:

1. Anthropos (The Man);
2. Anthropos, Son of Anthropos (Man, Son of Man);
3. Ildabaoth (The Son of Chaos.)

Ildabaoth, who corresponds to Zeus in the Orphic and Platonic metaphysics, is called the Demiurgus or Lord of the World. The Gnostics believe that it was this Demiurgus to whom Jesus referred when he spoke of the Prince of this World, who had nothing in common with him. The Demiurgus was the personification of matter, the Monad of the material sphere with all its mass of sidereal phenomena. Ildabaoth gave birth out of himself to six sons who, together with their father, became the seven planetary spirits. These were called the Seven Archons and correspond to the Guardians of the World described by Hermes. Their names and order, according to Origen, are as follows:

1. Ildabaoth (Saturn);
2. Eloi (Jupiter);
3. Sabaoth (Mars);
4. Adonai (Sun);
5. Orai (Venus);
6. Astaphai (Mercury);
7. Tao (Moon).

In the Hermetic allegory, the Seven Guardians of the World —the Builders or Elohim of the Jews—were simply manifestors of divine purpose, in themselves neither good nor bad. According to the Gnostics, however, Ildabaoth and his six sons were proud and opposing spirits who, like Lucifer and his rebels, sought to establish a kingdom in the Abyss which should prevail against the kingdom of God. Hence we find Ildabaoth crying out triumphantly, "There are no other gods before me," when in reality he is the least part of the triune Godhead and beyond him extend the spheres of the Father and the Son.

From this brief summary it will be evident that Gnosticism is a restatement of the eternal doctrine of the warfare that must exist in space between spirit and matter. Life, on the one hand, struggling against the encroachment of form, and form, on the other hand, strangling out the breath of life, is a concept that underlies nearly every great religious system of mankind. The Gnostics evidently intended to interpret the incarnation of Jesus as equivalent to the tenth, or Kalki, Avatar of Vishnu. The Avatara theme is a very ancient one, and in every case is the account of a divine personality temporarily descending into the sphere of matter to accomplish the redemption of a relapsed humanity. In the Bhagavad-Gita, the Avatar Krishna says, "When virtue fails upon the earth, then I come forth."

Matter is the eternal adversary, and Ildabaoth and his six sons are the seven deadly sins of theology which, by the enlightenment of the soul, are transmuted into the seven cardinal virtues. When regarded from an absolutely neutral standpoint, the seven Archons are the liberal arts and sciences, or even the seven senses. These are battles in space in which spirit and matter struggle for supremacy over attitudes, ideals, and purposes.

Gnostic Christianity conceived of salvation without benefit of clergy. Christ, the Sotar, was the high priest who by his descent had destroyed the whole of the old order of things. Religion became a matter of internal adjustment. Forms and rituals by which primitive peoples had propitiated Ildabaoth were regarded as rendered valueless by the resurrection of the Christos. The rule of fear and doubt was gone; the rule of love and charity had come. The Church, however, regarded this new order of things as economically unsound. Love frees; fear enslaves. So the Gnostics were destroyed lest they free men from bondage to the priestcraft.

*QUESTION—What effect did the destruction of the Alexandrian Library have on occult knowledge?*

*Answer*—It is generally acknowledged that the ancient Egyptians possessed an extraordinary knowledge of the arts and sciences. Their earliest pharaohs were patrons of learning in all its branches. Their priests and philosophers were the most scholarly of men. The architecture of the Egyptians has awed the world for fifty centuries, and their wisdom in chemistry, anatomy, medicine and astronomy was no less amazing.

Under the dynasty of the Ptolemies, the city of Alexandria became a Mecca for scholars. The studious of all nations congregated there to enjoy unparalleled opportunities for mental self-improvement. Poets, historians, philosophers and dramatists assembled in the city of the Ptolemies largely to consult the vast libraries that had been accumulated by the pharaohs of this illustrious line.

Knowledge, like a magnet, draws more knowledge to itself, and by the second century before the Christian era, the city of Alexandria became a veritable metropolis of books. Its libraries are referred to in ancient documents as the glory of the world—the axis of the intellectual universe. In addition to numerous private libraries collected by specialists in various departments of learning, and the secret collections written in the hieratic glyphs of the priests, there were two immense public collections. The largest of these was the Brucheum which formed a branch of the national Museum of Antiquities, and contained some 490,000 papyri, vellums, tablets and inscriptions, magnificently arranged in the niches and wings of a great rotunda-like gallery.

The second and smaller public collection, devoted almost exclusively to obscure forms of knowledge, and therefore probably of greater practical value, was contained in the Temple of Serapis, the patron deity of the Ptolemies. This building, called Serapeum, housed 42,800 rolls, preserved in fireproof containers shaped somewhat like buckets with tightly fitted lids. The various private collections brought the total number of priceless literary treasures in Alexandria to a figure exceeding one million.

It is difficult to compare this ancient collection with any modern library. Many institutions of the present day contain a larger number of books, as for example the British Museum, which has over seventy miles of bookshelves. But modern collections are mostly printed books of which there are numerous copies, comparatively inexpensive and easily secured. The Alexandrian collection was made up entirely of handwritten works, for the most part unique copies of the greatest antiquity, each of which today would be worth a king's ransom. There is not enough money in the world to buy the Alexandrian library if it existed today. When we realize that one 4th-century Greek manuscript, the Codex Sinaiticus, is now being purchased by the British Museum for half a million dollars, we get some idea of their values.

The fate of the Alexandrian libraries is one of the greatest tragedies of history. In the first century B. C., Cleopatra contested with a brother for the throne of Egypt. Caesar ordered the burning of the fleet in the harbor of Alexandria. A strong wind rose, the fire reached the docks and spread. Before the conflagration could be checked, it destroyed the Brucheum and the greater part of the city. When Cleopatra entered Alexandria, under the favor of Caesar, she ordered herself carried to the ruins of the great library. The old accounts tell that she beheld a veritable mountain of charred manuscripts and rolls, and the Queen of the Sun cursed her ancestors that they had not made adequate provision to protect the library from fire. The burning of the Brucheum was regarded by the Egyptians as a national disaster, and by way of atonement Rome presented to Cleopatra several valuable collections of manuscripts which it had accumulated from conquered peoples. Mark Antony was especially active in the restoration of the Brucheum.

The great Alexandrian libraries were a second time destroyed by Aurelian about 273 A.D. The Serapeum was completely razed by the Christians in 389 A.D. by the Edict of Theodosius. The colossal statue of the weeping god Serapis, which stood in the middle of the Serapeum, was also demolished at this time. Alexandria never entirely recovered from this third catastrophe. The love of learning lingered on, however, until the last of the great collections was entirely wiped out by Amru the Saracen in 640 A.D. Thus perished the glory of the world, the sanctuary of the arts and sciences, mother of wisdom.

If we were asked to estimate what humanity has lost through the destruction of the Alexandrian libraries, we need only to say that after Alexandria came the Dark Ages—the total eclipse of essential learning. Today a hundred branches of art and science, philosophy and religion, are laboring patiently and painfully to restore a body of knowledge that perished at the hands of ignorance and vandalism. The lost arts and sciences, the secrets of everlasting pigments, the mystery of malleable glass, the ever-burning lamps, and the transmutation of metals, are among the minor losses. The greater tragedy is the loss of the histories of the antediluvian world— the beginnings of civilization—the origin of races, philosophies, religions and sciences—the secrets and accumulated knowledge of the lost Atlantis—and the story of its final destruction, when, according to the Troano Codex of the Mayans, it sank some ten to twelve thousand years ago, carrying sixty million souls to death in a single night.

Thus the most precious secrets of human origin, to which we have recovered only the faintest clues, vanished away in smoke. Serapis, the sorrowful god, had the literature of a thousand generations for a funeral pyre.

But wisdom did not entirely die with the burning of its shrine. According to Theodas, faithful librarians and priests rescued a few of the most priceless of the manuscripts, hiding them in various places, and secreting a considerable number in underground temples in the Sahara desert. Our great libraries and museums probably include among their various collections some mutilated fragments of this old collection that came to light in various excavations. But the important parts, if preserved, have not yet been rediscovered by the modern world.

*QUESTION—What are the qualifications for discipleship in the Mystery Schools?*

*Answer—*In occult philosophy, the term *discipleship* means a student who is under the personal supervision of an accredited teacher of metaphysical philosophy. Discipleship must follow an extensive period of studentship and probationship. Such probationary preparation usually requires from five to ten years, but under no condition is probationship determined by time, rather by the aptitude and advancement of the student. In the Eastern schools, the disciples live with their teachers, usually in the capacity of servants, performing without question or reservation any task he may order. In the Western schools of the Classical period, each disciple was appointed a teacher and studied with him usually from five to fifteen years. At the end of whatever period necessary, the master conferred upon his disciple the esoteric secrets of his order, and the disciple then became a full-fledged teacher himself. Even after receiving the arcana, or secrets, and becoming himself a teacher, the disciple remained always in the relationship of a pupil to the particular master from whom he had received instruction. This relationship continued until the master's death.

In modern metaphysics, discipleship is very difficult of attainment in the Western world, for the reason that the old schools have vanished from Western society. It would be incorrect, however, to say that it is impossible to achieve discipleship in the West, because highly advanced probationers are usually brought into contact with proper instruction when they are ready to receive it. The reason so few Western students of mysticism ever get anywhere is because they cannot successfully pass the tests of probationship. These tests not only involve a high standard of living and thinking, and a dedication to the ideals of mysticism, but a special cultivation of practical common sense. The majority of students in the Western world fail because they wander off to worship at the altars of strange gods and are imposed upon by the innumerable shysters and charlatans in the field of modern occult sciences. "Falling sickness" is the most serious disease of the truth seeker. He is always "falling" for some strange unreasonable cult or for some silly pseudo-revelation that has nothing in it of real or permanent value. The student who cannot avoid unfortunate affiliations evidently lacks the discrimination that would fit him for acceptance by a real esoteric school.

Probationship in the West is a voluntary dedication to mystical discipline. It brings with it a deluge of problems

and responsibilities. If the probationer cannot master circumstances and prove his strength, he must wait until another
life and try again. Two or three "backslidings" in one life
make achievement in that life very improbable. But each
new incarnation brings with it greater strength and greater
intelligence out of the experiences of the past, and in the
end each soul succeeds. The essence of the matter is not
speed, but thoroughness.

Briefly stated, the requirements of discipleship are: a high
standard of personal integrity, a good development of the
faculty of discrimination, a well-rounded background in the
literature, culture and ethics of metaphysics, and an indom-
itable courage to sacrifice the lesser for the greater. There
must be physical, emotional and mental control and direction,
and an abundance of constructive patience. All attitudes must
be impersonalized; inordinate attachments must be overcome;
and the life must be dedicated to the transmutation of the
lower nature and the practice of the virtues. Discipleship is
the living of the philosophic life, and when this has been
accomplished, there is nothing that can prevent the disciple
from being accepted by a teacher of one of the branches of
the esoteric schools.

*QUESTION—Give a practical definition of mysticism.*

*Answer*—There are three terms in common use among
metaphysicians that should receive exact definition. Exoteric-
ally speaking, occultism is the intellectual approach to truth;
mysticism is the emotional approach to truth; and psychism
is the physical approach to truth. Esoterically, the occultist
desires to possess wisdom; the mystic desires to be possessed
by wisdom; and the psychic, incapable of impersonalizing

wisdom, seeks to achieve a spiritual state by permitting his own metaphysical organism to be controlled by other entities, by this process hoping to benefit by the experience of others. Practical mysticism may be defined as the intuitional grasp of reality. The practical mystic is one whose outer life is regulated by the beauty, gentleness, and sublimity of inward conviction. Mysticism is the sublimation of emotion. The Buddhist would define it as the transmutation of passions into compassions, the elevation of attachments from a level of particulars to the level of impersonals.

*QUESTION—How can we contact the Masters or a teacher of the wisdom religion?*

*Answer*—We cannot too strongly caution truth seekers against a frenzied running around in search of Mahatmas. Every few years the "adept" craze breaks out again. All the great Mystery Schools have taught the existence of highly perfected human beings, but these schools have also warned their students not to be deceived by charlatans who come in the name of truth. It is lamentable in the extreme that thousands of people every year must be the victims of religious imposture. Fortunately, this imposture is not necessary, and to be completely deceived a student must be a party to his own deception.

Among the axioms of Hermes is one that all neophytes should remember: "When the disciple is ready, the Master is there." It is evident from this that when the disciple is *not* ready, there is no master. Thus the whole issue is really a very simple one.

If people could only be convinced of their own failings, and further convinced that their first spiritual duty is to cor-

rect these failings, the Mahatma craze would end "aborning."
There is nothing more absolutely and inconceivably ridiculous
than a large group of people who know nothing about themselves, about life, or about nature, listening in at one end of
a private wire with the Infinite. As the average person would
not know a Mahatma if he saw one, it is not difficult to convince him that almost anyone whom he meets might be a
Mahatma. It is also quite useless to pray to Mahatmas or
to feel that some exalted body of superhuman beings is going
to multiply the contents of one's purse, cure one's aches and
pains, or bestow upon one a powerful and convincing personality.

The law of karma, or cause and effect, is absolute. No
Mahatma, even if he so desired, could transform a fool into
a philosopher. All the adepts in the universe cannot prevent
a foolish person from reaping his follies. Mahatmas do not
deal in real estate, vicarious atonement, or love philters. Nor
do they give any human being the right to promise in their
names anything that is contrary to the laws of nature.

The path of discipleship is a path of gradual growth and
consecration to idealism. The average person must spend
*many lives* in preparation before he can expect to be given
advance instruction by one of the masters of wisdom. Long
before he is ready for such instruction, he has renounced
the physical world and its illusions. He no longer desires
wealth and power and platitudes. He no longer holds out his
purse to be blessed, and he no longer sits agape at the feet
of miracle-mongers. Such tactics belong to tiny little hysterical
souls who have glimpsed but little of the Light that sustains
the world.

The coming of a teacher has been well described by one
of the alchemical philosophers of the 18th century. This

consecrated and enlightened soul explained that for nearly fifty years he sought diligently for the Wise Man's Stone (Truth). He mastered arts and sciences, he grew step by step, his entire life dedicated to the highest ideals. Each discovery that he made, he gave to the world. As a physician he healed the sick, and the halt, the lame and the blind made a path to his door. He asked nothing and he gave all, preserving with the depth of his knowledge the gentleness of his spirit.

He relates that one day as he worked in his laboratory (life) seeking for the medicine of human ills (wisdom) a voice spoke to him. He turned, and there beside him stood a traveler (a sage). The stranger wore the simple garb of the country and bore a pack on his back (knowledge). In a few words he revealed to the alchemist (spiritual chemist) the secret he desired to know. Then, without bothering to open the door, the stranger disappeared. The alchemist fell on his knees and gave thanks to God, and then rising hastily began to perfect the experiment, mindful of the needs of others. He never saw the stranger again.

Such is a true story of a prepared student who was given that which he was prepared to receive. When man, by virtue of his own merit, is in need of instruction, no power in heaven or earth can come between him and that which he merits. Until he is ready, no power on earth or in heaven can give him a knowledge of which he is not capable or worthy.

Adepts come only to individuals, for no group of people simultaneously merits the same instruction. Nor does any adept send one exclusive messenger to bear witness of him. The adepts serve all who need them and are ready for their instructions. They have no favorites or "spiritual pets." The student who desires to contact an adept must place himself under rigid discipline for many years, and hope by this process to develop qualities which the Great School will find useful to its work. To restate once more the true formula that should be made part of the life of every true aspirant: "When the disciple is ready, the Master is there."

QUESTION—*Do you advocate joining organizations and brotherhoods promulgating certain religious, philosophical codes? If so, kindly give the names of such sects and groups as you can recommend.*

*Answer*—This question must be considered from several angles. In the first place, it has often been said that in organization there is strength. But is it not also true that this strength is of the organization, and not of the individual? Groups of people—either in communities or in organizations—depending upon each other for mutual support and mutual enlightenment, all too often lose both their individuality and their independence. Thus while the strength of the entire group is continually increased by new recruits, it is a question just what effect is produced upon the recruit.

In the second place, motive is the deciding factor in many of these problems. Why does an individual join an organization? Is his purpose to lean upon or to be leaned upon? If he is weak, he will lean upon any strong personality with whom he comes in contact; and if he is strong, it will not be long before the greater part of an organization will be leaning upon him, and he will be denounced by that vast number of leaners as they become envious of his intelligence, if he possesses any. Most people who join religious and philosophical organizations do so for what they can get, and not for what they can give; and a large group, composed of individuals with axes to grind, has very little to offer to an active, independent intellect.

In the third place, organizations have a habit of being inconsistent and inconstant in their doctrines. Today you may be able to vouch for everything they do; tomorrow their policies may be widely at variance with your ideals. Most organizations, moreover, do not contain more than one real mind. This mind is reflected in the membership. When this individual mind changes its opinions, the membership—chameleon-like—changes its mental and spiritual shades to match the background. Those who will not change, branch out, and form a new society. Finally what was once a single train of thought and purpose becomes a seven-headed Hydra with all the heads biting at one another.

In the fourth place, organizations are segregative and separative. If you join an organization, the world considers you as championing the doctrines and codes promulgated by that group with which you have associated yourself. The saddest part of this feature is that the world also considers you as being opposed to and irreconcilably against those other organizations and individuals whose ideals are at variance with the cult that you have accepted. In other words, the world says that if you are for one thing, you must be against all else; or, if actual animosity does not exist, there must be at least a dangerous indifference.

In the fifth place, it is a well known fact that crystallization is the keynote of the physical world and vitalization the keynote of the spiritual world. Organizations seemingly cannot exist without crystallization, which gradually produces in spiritual movements the same conditions that it produces in the physical body: age, disease, suffering and death. Death is the separation of conscious life from a vehicle no longer capable of giving it expression. All spiritual truths die when their vehicles become crystallized, and no organization has yet been formed that has been able to escape the inevitable dissolution resulting from crystallization. If the organization could die without involving the individuals who compose it, things would not be so bad. When the mind has followed and accepted dogma and creed for a certain length of time, it becomes incapable of individual estimation, and the decay of the organization—by destroying the crutch upon which those lean who have lost the power to stand alone—leaves its component parts hopeless, helpless, and useless.

In the sixth place, the modern world lacks the solidarity of antiquity. We are a generation of superficial thinkers, and therefore the products of our thought are superficial and impermanent. The organizations and institutions of antiquity stood for centuries because their founders and members represented the highest types of intellect. The ranks of the ancient educational and spiritual orders were not composed of easy believers. Each member dared to think his own thoughts, live his own life, and doubt anything that did not seem reasonable to his senses. Ancient religion was not a process of acceptance; every theory advanced was discussed, and accepted or rejected upon the basis of its intrinsic merit. If modern organizations were of standards comparable to those of the ancients, they would be of vastly greater value, although, being organizations, they must meet the inevitable fate of organizations—crystallization. Modern cults are all too often the brainstorms of honest but mentally incompetent persons who, fired with aspiration but lacking logic, reason, and philosophical education, are not properly qualified to finish the task they have begun.

In the seventh place, unfortunately we are living in an age of commercialism, which has as surely permeated our philosophical world as it has our material sphere. A great number of cults and creeds have been foisted upon the public, not by philosophers and mystics, but by financiers. Many of these have been eminently successful, as the disillusioned members will testify after the bubble has burst. In this respect, it may be truthfully said that the devil has quoted Scripture with profit. Indeed, it has become quite a problem now to decide, when joining an organization, whether it will lead you to heaven or to the poor-farm.

In the eighth place, spiritual and philosophical societies are the breeding grounds for the most dangerous form of hero-worship. It is positively amazing to note how quickly half a dozen foolish people can make a demigod out of a seventh poor sinner. It is our firm belief that no person who ever worshipped a man understood him. Nearly all groups of people seem concerned with the perpetual deification of some poor, hard-working, long-suffering being who may have died of starvation, whose words are quoted as Scripture, and whose accomplishments form the axis of the organization.

Having considered the arguments against affiliation with religious and philosophic organizations, it is only fair to present the other side of the proposition. There are two outstanding reasons why affiliation with the right kind of a group may attain a definite and constructive end:

1. In an age that organizes and incorporates all forms of activity, it is almost impossible for religion, philosophy, and ethics to survive unless they combat material organization with spiritual organizations. Single individuals are overwhelmed by the mass movement of a materially organized civilization. Unless those interested in maintaining the high

standards of culture absolutely indispensable to the survival of the race, pool their strength, modern commercialism may totally obliterate creative idealism.

2. Man's mind is tremendously influenced by what takes place about him. A child will study more faithfully at school than at home, because in the schoolroom there are numbers of other children doing the same thing. There is also a certain amount of vanity involved. No individual likes to exhibit less capacity and intelligence than the person next to him. Thus, organization offers a twofold incentive for greater accomplishment: the stimulus of environment and the stimulus of personal vanity.

There are several organizations of a philosophic, religious and fraternal nature in America and in other parts of the world that are actually accomplishing a great amount of good. Our position does not permit us to actually name them, nor could we conscientiously assume the personal responsibility of deflecting the mind of another person into any prescribed channel of thought and activity. Therefore, we can only suggest that in matters pertaining to organization, an acid test be applied. We will suppose that you feel an inner urge to associate yourself with some group interested in philosophic or religious studies. You should investigate the matter very carefully, realizing that, in all probability, many of your future actions will be influenced by the code promulgated by that particular cult.

Do not be in haste to join new movements that have not had an opportunity for time to pass upon their merits. Time is the heartless critic, continually denouncing and exposing weakness, falseness and inconsistency. On the other hand, do not condemn that which is new, but, restraining both enthusiasm and criticism, judge all things by their works.

There are good organizations, bad organizations, and indifferent organizations. Good ones are in every case progressive, altruistic, educational, non-commercial, and impersonal. They seek to build individual character, teaching men *how* to think rather than *what* to think.

Bad organizations are usually non-progressive, penurious, bigoted, commercial, and personal. They are usually built up about some individual who believes that he can increase his own power and position by having an organization behind him. In many cases, such individuals depend upon superstition for the attainment of their ends. They have long and curious names, weird and hair-raising mysteries. They conceal themselves behind a barrage of meaningless bombast, so that those entering the cult cannot get close enough to find out how little the great man knows!

Indifferent organizations are those which, being neither hot nor cold, meet the sad fate prescribed for such: "the Lord speweth them out of His mouth."

If you desire to join an organization for spiritual or ethical betterment, feeling that you have not yet reached the place where you are qualified to decide for yourself that which is best for your immortal soul, we suggest that you search out a group as loosely organized as possible, for many a noble enterprise has been hobbled by its own red tape. Go to an organization that makes no profession that it is wiser or greater than others but, in modesty and simplicity, is diligently striving to work out the problems of life. Shun, as you would the plague, deep and profound secrets, unutterable mysteries, and ten-dollar admission fees. Beware of mechanical cults that grind out "initiates" and "illumination" courses. If possible, find a group that is promulgating the ancient systems of philosophy and thought. Eschew exclusiveness, and permit yourself to be involved in nothing that is not big enough to recognize the good in all men, the wisdom in all religious systems, and the fact that truth belongs to no man. Beware, most of all, of any group or cult that is the self-appointed and sole custodian of truth, for all who believe they are the only ones to whom God has communicated his divine knowledge, brand themselves as false prophets.

# HUMAN REGENERATION

## PART SIX

*QUESTION—What is the Fall of Man?*

*Answer*—It is still the belief of millions of members of the Christian Church that the fall of Adam was the original sin that must taint every human being who is born into this world. In spite of the advantages of education and the increasing standard of individual integrity, innumerable theologians are still ranting about Adam's fall and the apple in Eden's garden. Seemingly, it has never occurred to these brothers of the cloth that the story of Adam might have a mystical or philosophical meaning very different from the literal implications.

The word *Adam,* meaning *species* or *type,* signifies humanity collectively; that is, the wave of cosmic life that is now flowing through nature in the form of human beings. Adam is the protagonist, the archetypal or collective human idea. The Garden of Eden is the etheric sphere that surrounds the earth, the humidic world that was the abode of man before he descended into the experience of physical existence. Ether is called by the alchemists the quintessence, or the fifth essence, a spiritual substance from which the four elements are differentiated. These are symbolized in the Biblical account of the four rivers that flow out of Eden. The very

161

physical body of the earth was precipitated out of the etheric substances.

When the organization of the earth's surface had been accomplished, waves of life descended from the ethers and took upon themselves physical form. It is this descent of spiritual beings into the earth's material nature that constituted the "fall." This fall was not the result of sin, but the soul's quest for experience. A young man starting out in life may leave the security of his own home to wander in the hazards of individual experience, and he may suffer deeply, go through extreme privation, but all these uncertainties and tribulations are necessary to the perfection of consciousness. In the same way, the human life wave flowed downward from the etheric paradise to become man, confronted with all the perplexities that beset man, and guilty of all of the mistakes that man makes. Yet all this is part of the beautiful necessity of life. Gradually, through the ages, the sublimity that is locked within man's mortal nature begins to shine through, revealing the splendor of the inner self. God-like men and women appear upon the earth, bearing witness to the godlikeness in all men.

In the parable of the Prodigal Son, the wanderer who went out into the experiences of life was more honored upon his return than his virtuous brother who had remained at home. Man is a fallen angel, and his wings are well concealed, but in time he will regain their use and soar upward again to the heights from which he came. By his experience in matter, man shall indeed be greater than the angels, for he will have that which can come only from the experiences of searching and finding. It was no great evil that man should fall from his etheric homeland; the evil lies in his failure to rise again.

When man took on his coat of skin and entered upon the mysterious course of racial unfoldment, he forgot the heights from which he had come, he forgot the purpose of living, and he forgot even the existence of his own inner soul. Now, after millions of years of growing up through the darkness in the obscurity of forms, man is beginning to discover himself. Dimly he perceives the purpose, and sets himself to the task of regaining his lost estate. Aspiration in the human heart is man yearning for the higher life that faded out when he assumed the illusion of material existence. The fallen angel is preparing to ascend again.

*QUESTION—Explain the theory of human regeneration.*

*Answer*—Man is a spiritual being exiled to a world of matter. The great schools of ancient philosophy all agree that the material state is not natural to the soul, but is assumed for the purposes of experience. The involuntary processes (described in the previous answer) drew spirit into form. Here the spiritual principles strive for equilibrium, producing the urge toward improvement, present at least potentially in all human beings. The urge to grow is present everywhere in nature. All creatures, from the least to the greatest, are unfolding or developing from within outwardly. In the human being the urge to improve is expressed rationally, and man puts his intellect to work to devise means of co-operating consciously with the evolutionary processes.

The arts, crafts, trades and sciences are rudimentary expressions of the urge to grow, to release abilities and capacities, and to perfect the instruments of judgment. But education does not end with the training of the mind or the skilling of the hands. Education continues, urging man relentlessly on toward the perfection of himself.

The intelligent man, realizing that the evolution of society is slowed down to accommodate the stragglers or the uninformed, founded systems of special instruction to assist advanced types. The result was the Mystery Schools, institutions that have appeared among all great civilizations. These schools developed systems of special culture intended to stimulate, train, and directionalize the metaphysical forces in the subjective nature of human beings. The formulas of these schools were called *disciplines.* The disciplines differed according to the requirements of various races and nations, but in all cases, the end to be achieved was identical—the release of the true man from the limitations imposed by material organisms and material nature.

The disciplines of the principal Mystery Schools can be classified under three general headings:

1. *Occult Disciplines.* Under this heading may be grouped all the formulas of occult development that are based upon special exercises or processes. The Hindu Yogas — Karma, Jnana and Raja—are examples of discipline directed toward the refining of the body by special exercises to increase the rate of vibration of the physical atoms, thus making them more responsive to impulses of the spiritual principles. The Tantric practices, Mantra and Mudra magic, and the reciting of sacred formulas, as the *Om mani padme hum* formula, come under the same heading. Breathing exercises, and the focussing of the mind on various parts of the body, in the effort to open spiritual centers or to raise the Kundalini, belong also under this classification. The occult exercises of meditation, concentration, retrospection, and the Taoist exer-

cises such as the multiplication of personality, are also aspects of occult disciplines.

2. *Philosophical Disciplines.* All systems of moral and ethical culture based upon man's co-operation through understanding are properly philosophical disciplines. Platonism is an excellent example of a philosophical system that lifts man up to the realization of truth through the unfoldment of rationality. The inner life is released by putting the outer life in order. Buddhism is another example of a philosophical discipline accomplishing the purposes of a religion. As the Greeks expressed it, learning draws the soul gently from the body. For all beginners in occultism, the philosophical disciplines are the safest method of approach. Man is never injured by learning, but he can be seriously injured if he attempts to stimulate occult forces that he cannot control.

3 *Esthetic Disciplines.* Esthetics is founded upon the releasing, perfecting power of beauty. The arts, by cultivating the love of beauty, refine the individual. Of all the arts, the art of living beautifully is the highest. The end of esthetics is to contribute the refining, redeeming power to every thought and action of life. Through outward grace achieving inward grace, man approaches God. Ritual and ceremony are factors in esthetic discipline. The impressiveness of the great cathedral, the beauty of fine painting, the inspiring voices of a great choir, all these are esthetic factors in religion. They restate the significance of spiritual things by presenting truth dramatically and beautifully. From the earliest time, man has adorned the places of his worship with the highest expressions of his art. In India, the rock-hewn temples are adorned with the most exquisite carving. In Siam, the temple dancers honor the gods with patterns and postures cultivated for thousands of years. The Pythagoreans met the dawn with hymns and

dancing to the soft voices of the lutes. Everywhere, man has found expression for his religious emotions through art; and everywhere, art born of religion has inspired man to higher personal standards of action.

Whatever discipline man may choose, he desires as a consummation of it the release of the truth within himself. He longs to go forth out of the small into the great, out of the narrow house of his own body to the larger house which is the body of God. He realizes that only by improving himself can he rise above the illusions of the material world. This improvement can come only as the result of self-mastery and self-mastery can come only from self-discipline. Therefore discipline is the beginning, and man discovers that in conquering himself, he masters the whole world. Human regeneration is the intelligent man setting himself to the task of releasing his spiritual nature from bondage to the instincts and appetites of the animal nature.

*QUESTION—Is celibacy essential to spiritual development?*

*Answer*—Most of the great religious systems of the world have sponsored monastic orders, have placed their stamp of approval on the doctrine of religious celibacy or, more correctly, chastity. Christianity, which is the principal religious factor in the background of Western people, from the beginning advocated extreme asceticism as the surest way to escape the corrupting force of the "flesh and the devil." Several of the early fathers of the Church advanced the hope that the universal acceptance of the vows of chastity would speedily bring about the depopulation of the earth and the end of mortal suffering. Monastic orders have flourished in China, India, Greece, Egypt, in fact in practically all advanced systems of civilization; but in each case, only a certain type of humanity found solace or enlightenment through affiliation with them.

Protestant Christianity broke away from many of the dogmas of the old church. The problem of celibacy was a major equation in the Reformation. Experience showed that not even the clergy flourished consistently under vows of chastity, and Martin Luther raised his voice strongly against the imposing of such strict regulations upon the lives of mortals. It was the medieval experience that the increase of monastic orders brought with it problems no end. General reforms were eventually necessary, and Protestantism is, in reality, only reformed Catholicism stripped of certain extreme attitudes but still permeated with the old psychology.

Modern metaphysical organizations, deriving most of their authority from the past, are naturally concerned with the issue of celibacy, and students of metaphysics all over the world are trying to decide, in their own way, the correct interpretation of the philosophic maxim of moderation and sanity. Strictly speaking, asceticism and chastity are not identical terms, for asceticism is a large, inclusive term, and chastity is only one of its inferences. Asceticism is a complete renunciation of personal existence. The ascetic retires from life and all its material emphasis, to devote his heart and mind to an uninterrupted contemplation of spiritual truths. Asceticism is renunciation of things and thoughts. It is natural at a certain stage of evolution, and is right only when it is natural. Correctly speaking, the ascetic is not one who takes obligations, but one whose very life is naturally detached from the extremes of physical life. The true ascetic is born, not made, and under such conditions, there is no conflict, no struggle to live up to something that is constantly in combat with appetites and desires.

Asceticism is not suitable to the average metaphysician whose degree of spiritual development is extremely dubious and whose attachments to life are both real and intense. Asceticism is not suitable to the individual who must live in community existence and fight desperately for economic survival, and whose life is a constant struggle, dominated by ambitions and responsibilities. Nor is chastity successful as the only virtue or the dominant virtue in life. It cannot be successful when it is in conflict with the normalcy of the individual. Strictly speaking, it is one of the most advanced of the metaphysical disciplines and is suitable only to highly advanced types. For the rest, it is a stupid blunder.

Self-discipline begins in small matters, and, with the unfolding of consciousness, increases in depth and intensity. Discipline is not the individual forcing himself to do something he does not want to do; rather, it is inner conviction directing outer action. Discipline is living up to what one knows and not forcing oneself to live beyond this understanding and capacity. Only when all the thoughts and emotions have been brought to a high degree of moderation can the monastic life be assumed with any probability of success. Man does not escape either the temptations or responsibilities of life by running away from them to some secluded cloister. Rather, each individual must master life by the development of an inner strength that bestows sufficiency and the courage of enlightened action.

Religion has an unpleasant habit of meddling in the personal problems of people, when it should be far above all petty concerns, dedicated to the great and enduring principles. Many modern metaphysical movements try to impose celibacy upon a diversified membership, with the most disastrous results. Butchers, bakers, and candlestick makers develop the monastic complex, and though bound to physical life by every thought and emotion, they decide that inhibition is the road to glory. In fact, the decision is thrust upon them. A few years of study of metaphysical abstractions does not insure the ascetic qualifications. When chastity is advocated for all men of mankind, only the gravest misfortune can result. The average individual is simply unfitted for, and psychologically unsuited to, such a course of procedure.

Remember, as spirituality is truth coming out of one it is not one's personal ambition trying to force abstractions upon oneself. Right thought, right emotion, and right action so refine the outer life that ever more of inward reality shines through, enlightening, perfecting, and inspiring. One cannot kill out worldliness by violent effort, but worldliness dies out in those who have worked through it and finished the lessons it has to teach.

While it is undoubtedly true that the great initiates and adepts have reached that point in their evolution where all physical attachments and physical emotions have been sublimated, it is a serious mistake for beginners in metaphysics to pattern their actions after the Mahatmas without having the inner enlightenment and inner security that come with great spiritual advancement. Many people overestimate their own enlightenment. They believe themselves to be highly advanced and on the very verge of cosmic consciousness, when in reality they have not reached even a reasonable degree of ordinary intelligence. People go about asking for the secret of illumination, who are unable to make any important intelligent decision in life. Neither educated, cultured, nor informed; neither wise, understanding, nor controlled, these well-meaning but foolish individuals are fully convinced that if they breathe right, eat right, or devoutly inhibit themselves, universal comprehension will descend upon them and they will gain all without *being* anything. Extreme ascetic discipline for such people would be moral suicide. They are not ready for it, not even capable of understanding it, and certainly biologically unfitted for it. The fires have not died out; they have merely been suppressed in an heroic effort to assume the appearance of virtue. Well-meaning, perhaps, but ineffectual.

From a practical standpoint, then, we may say the vow of chastity is unnecessary to most truth seekers at their present state of evolution. In fact it would be almost impossible for them to live consistently even the doctrine of moderation. Nor is it at all likely that in their present incarnation these truth seekers will be greatly handicapped in their aspirations by well-regulated and moderate human relationships. There are numerous examples to prove that even a high degree of spirituality has been attained without extreme asceticism.

To review the facts briefly: Confucius was married and the father of children; Buddha, possibly the most highly evolved of human beings, passed through the experience of marriage and fatherhood but later renounced these relationships for the ascetic life. There is no evidence that his family relationship interfered finally with his illumination. His departure from human ties was not forced, but was the result of his own decision, based upon the deepest and most enlightened realization of his own peculiar work and ministry. Zoroaster was the father of several children, yet is included among the great world saviors, and was the founder and head of one of the deepest of the ancient schools. Pythagoras married one of his own disciples, was the father of children, and his wife continued his school after his martyrdom. Mohammed was married, his wife Khadijah being his first convert, and he was survived by one daughter. Hermes dedicated some of his deepest sermons to his son Tatian. Akhnaton, the first mystic recorded in history, is shown in the ancient carvings with his wife Nefertiti and their children. This list could be increased indefinitely, and seems to indicate that the average individual has no cause to worry about family relationships preventing his usefulness and attainment. A list could also be built up of great mystics who chose the ascetic life. Proof can therefore be advanced to favor either side of the argument, but there is abundant evidence that human beings can be great, noble, and good, and still not retire entirely from social life. Certainly it is not necessary, nor advisable, to break up homes, possibly doing a deep and lasting injury to others, merely in a selfish desire to attain enlightenment at the expense of personal responsibility.

We often wonder what would have happened to the world if the parents of the great philosophers and world teachers had chosen courses of celibacy, and in their personal sanctification had prevented the incarnation of these great souls. In practical terms, there is no one better fitted to give protection and opportunity to highly evolved souls than deeply informed and deeply serious people who are trying to live well and think well. The ancient Brahmans regarded it as personal selfishness to avoid the family responsibility, though to grow out of it after the responsibility had been met honestly and completely, was a spiritual virtue. Selfishness is never really philosophical, and those who think of their own spirituality are usually not as really spiritual as those who think first of their collective responsibilities and try to fulfill honestly and wisely each of the duties of life.

Let us say, therefore, that it is virtuous to moderate, dignify, and purify human relationships; that from the excess of ignorance we shall grow to the moderation of wisdom. Having brought all things to a moderate and ennobled plan, then and then only can the mind contemplate higher asceticism. Human society is built around the family relationship; the survival of society depends upon the family relationship; and the spiritual unfoldment of society depends upon the purification of the family relationship. The merit of right action is not to be ignored. Even the so-called advanced metaphysician has much to live up to, much to perfect, and much to purify, before the issue of the ascetic life is vital or imminent.

QUESTION—*Is ambition for spiritual advancement ethical or proper?*

*Answer*—The driving force of ambition is entirely inconsistent with spiritual aspiration. It is impossible to "storm the gates of heaven," and people who think of nothing but the advancement of their spiritual status are for the most part self-centered and disagreeable. In modern metaphysics, there has developed a hierarchy of "old souls," as fine a collection of Pharisees as ever disgraced the good name of religion. Neglecting the responsibilities of daily living, surrounded by a miasma of pernicious piety, and totally indifferent to the spiritual and temporal rights of others, these metaphysical nuisances may be best described as "hell-bent for heaven."

It is right and proper that spiritual progress should be the highest aspiration of the enlightened human being. But spiritual progress is a gentle, natural growing up to light. Jacob Boehme, the German mystic, likened the unfolding of the human soul to the opening of a flower that grows up beautifully in the light, injuring nothing, and untouched by the corrupting influence of pride.

There are several pertinent references in the Christian Bible which the "aristocracy" of metaphysicians would do well to ponder. Humility and true superiority are always found together. As man grows wiser, he realizes more fully how little he can know and how insignificant he is. As the Scriptures say, "He that thinketh he standeth, take heed lest he fall." And, "He who would be the greatest among you, let him be the servant of all."

Ambition cannot be completely divorced from pride and self-seeking. The soul that is capable of the conceit of self-ishness is incapable of perceiving the Real. Philosophy teaches man not that he shall be great or that he shall be good, or that he may possess the virtues or achieve to high estate. Philosophy teaches, rather, that by the living of the mystical life, the human being becomes not great in himself, but only a channel or instrument through which universal good may flow into the world. When the true mystic has come close to truth, his only possible emotion is humility. Self ceases in the service of the Real. He no longer cares whether or not he is anything. He is absorbed in a realization greater than himself and, in self-forgetfulness, finds peace.

*QUESTION—How can we develop discrimination?*

*Answer*—According to the philosophy of the Greeks, man occupies a middle position in the sphere of consciousness—suspended between the extremes of perfect wisdom, truth or realization, above, and ignorance, darkness or error, below. In the thought of the Chinese, the universe consists of heaven, earth, and man: heaven above, earth below, and man partakes in certain measure of both superior and inferior. Plato and Confucius agree perfectly that man possesses within himself a moving power, the active capacity to verge at will toward either of the extremes by which he is bounded. Evolution, in classical philosophy, is man unfolding toward the superior. In the teaching of the ancient wisdom, the positive instruments of this unfoldment are the laws of reincarnation and karma. By these laws, man is inevitably moved toward consciousness and away from ignorance, which, in the philosophical analysis, is the absence of sufficient awareness.

Discipline is the first requisite of the philosophic life. Discipline is self-imposed direction or control. The impulse toward improvement may arise from either an inward urge or from the comparisons of the outward life. Probably the first impulse toward improvement comes from contact with things of a superior nature. This contact inspires to greater personal effort, or shames one through the forced realization of personal inferiority. From discipline the life is gradually organized until a proper harmony of thought, emotion, and action frees the consciousness from the competitive strivings of temperamental excess, thus clarifying the viewpoint by impersonalizing the perspective.

Integrity is possible only to the impersonal thinker, for any violent attachment or aversion distorts perspective and leads to a whole philosophy or psychology of life in which the elements or parts are asymmetrically arranged. After all, man has to put his own world in order, and we use the term "his own world" with special meaning. Only perfect illumination can see the world as it really is. All partly developed entities must see the world as *they* are, and it is impossible for an unbalanced individual to have proper perspective. Our perceptions and our realizations tint, tone, color, or discolor our every contact with life and every impulse that flows into us through the sensory perceptions.

Discrimination cannot be that with which one starts, nor can it be assumed, or even developed, in a comparatively perfect form. It is like appreciation, skill, or discipline. It must develop gradually, in every way consistent with the general bodily, psychical and mental chemistry. Philosophy works from a number of fundamental premises. One of these is that balance or perspective is a product of disciplined control and the development of potential capacities. One man, moved by inner conviction, chooses to elevate himself or, as Plotinus says, "verge toward the good." He makes a decision. By a dedication to this decision, and usually with the aid of some system or discipline of philosophy, he develops himself through conscious effort. As he develops, discrimination inevitably results from development. The more one is, the more one knows, and discrimination is one of the highest forms of knowledge. Primitive man is protected by general codes and standards established in society, but as man outgrows society, he finds its laws no longer sufficient to protect him, and must depend upon himself not only for courage of conviction, but for intelligence of program.

In the thought of Porphyry, discrimination is abstinence, detachment, and the capacity to perceive the Beautiful. Socrates declared discrimination to be the skill in the inward intellect to choose always and cling to the One, the love of the Beautiful, and to do the Virtuous. Unfortunately, however, the standards of beauty, virtue, and integrity differ with the degree of evolution and the degree of discipline. Relatively speaking, discrimination is the power to do the best of that which is known, with the realization that the doing of the best increases the capacity to know. This increased capacity will in turn increase perspective. Empirically speaking, discrimination is the intellectual courage to choose from among all things that which is the final Good; but as the final Good is unknowable to that which has not achieved the ultimate in itself, discrimination always remains in practice the doing of the best that one knows.

It is an undeniable fact that all men know better than they do. It is this interval between inward standard and outward action—an interval of weakness, of fear, of doubt—that clearly shows lack of discipline and lack of devotion or dedication to principle. People constantly ask—"What shall I do?" Yet these very people contain the answer in themselves. The very urge to ask proves the presence of the answer. But man is always hoping that he will be told something more pleasant and easier than his own conviction. Simply stated, honest conviction leads to self-discipline. Self-discipline results in improvement. Improvement increases discrimination. And discrimination is the evidence of an acceptable unfoldment of self and, as the Greeks called it, the flowing of the individual into the universal, or the verging toward truth.

*QUESTION—What is the mystical experience?*

*Answer*—Havelock Ellis, the distinguished psychologist, in *The Dance of Life* describes what he terms a "mystical experience." This experience was a temporary extension of consciousness into universal values. For an instant, the inner and outer life assumed proper relationship to each other. That which was real assumed first place; that which was unreal was revealed as evident illusion. The inward consciousness that puts life in order may be termed a mystical experience.

Most people die without ever discovering what life really is. They float along on the surface of phenomenal existence, accepting without question the commonplace as the real. To accept the routine of eating, sleeping, and working as *life*, is to accept the lesser in the presence of the greater. To be satisfied even with learning, is to be less than the self. Yet the outside world, with its attachments and responsibilities, seems very near and very real; and the sphere of the sages, with its placid detachment, seems very distant and very difficult to accomplish. The mystical experience shows the error of this viewpoint. In reality it is the world that is far away, and the peace of the inner life that is very near.

To break up the old patterns of acceptance, and to live the inward life, is to rise victoriously above compromise and doubt. Yet this desirable end can be accomplished only when spiritual truths become realities to the personal consciousness. The mystical experience is the realization of the immanence of life, law and love. It is the realization that truth is closer to the individual than his environment, his body or his mind. It is also the realization that all the complicated circumstances of life are conspiring together toward the release of life from bondage to phenomena.

It never occurs to most people that education is preparation for only the physical life of the individual. One man spends a lifetime studying banking, another gives fifty years to surgery, and a third spends his life with the geologist's hammer. In the end, these three men are going to depart from this life to a larger universal existence in which banking, surgery, and geology have no significance. But from the mastery of physical sciences may come the potentials of understanding. All knowledge is unimportant in itself, but important in the inferences that may arise from it. The arts and sciences are all gateways to the temple of the cosmos, doors to the house of true learning. Each art and science leads in the end to God. The mystical experience is the binding together of what a man knows and building it into what he is. It is a realization that results from man's final distillation of experience. It is the instant of enlightenment that renders all things significant. It is man ensouling what he knows.

### QUESTION—*What is initiation?*

*Answer*—The word *initiation* actually means acceptance into a secret society and the arcana of that society. In occultism, initiation is acceptance into one of the secret schools of the occult sciences. For the modern truth seeker, initiation must be an inner experience, an inward unfoldment, resulting in a definite increase of knowledge and understanding.

Initiation is a student's conscious contact with the adepts and initiates of a bona fide Mystery School. True initiation implies conscious clairvoyance and a high degree of personal integrity and discipline. Any initiation, so-called, which is not preceded by an adequate period of discipleship and proper instruction, can have no metaphysical significance. All the rituals and ceremonials of ancient initiation are but symbolic of spiritual processes taking place in the unfolding organism of the sincere and intelligent disciple.

Students of metaphysics read marvelous accounts of the old Mystery temples in which, amidst solemn splendor, qualified candidates were raised into the light of truth. We would all like to join in the solemn processionals, bearing aloft the standards of our gods; we would like to hear the instructions given to the new initiates by the gloriously robed hierophant of the Mysteries. Great would be our joy if, Apuleiuslike, we could be carried through the elements and be brought face to face with the immortals. With the untrained mind, it is but one step from a fancy to a fact. The student reads of initiations far into the night, in sleep he dreams of them, and in the morning awakens convinced in his own mind that he has experienced a divine adventure. Those who dream of initiations to come, and long for that day when for them the heavens shall open and the mysteries of the soul be made clear, nearly all overlook a very important part of initiation rituals. In all such great systems as the Orphic, the Eleusinian, or the Mithraic, the ascent of man into the house of wisdom is preceded by his descent into the subterranean chambers of darkness, despair, and death. Years of suffering and preparation, hazards dangerous to life and limb, tests of the most exacting kind must be successfully passed by those who desire more knowledge than that which is the portion of ordinary folk.

The Druid neophytes of Britain and Gaul were sent out to sea in open boats without rudder or oars, left to the will of Providence. If they were not drowned, they were accepted as favored by Deity. In the Mithraic initiation, the neophyte was given a short and inadequate sword and sent alone into the darkness to fight wild beasts. In some of the Cretan rites, seekers after truth were left to wander for days, without food or water, in subterranean labyrinths where monstrous apparitions appeared to them and tested their courage at every step. Machinery has been found under the Egyptian temples, which reveals that the priests employed many mechanical devices to increase the hazards of the initiation rituals. Thus an unwary victim might suddenly find the floor open beneath him and his body hurled downward onto the upturned points of spears. Artificial torrents were loosed upon him to batter his body against the cavern walls; or in chambers especially prepared for that purpose, the walls would suddenly burst into flame, forcing the neophyte to actually dash through sheets of fire or be burned alive. Through all these tests, those who aspired to the higher truths were expected to remain calm and poised, to reason out their courses of procedure, and escape the pitfalls by the sheer force of intelligence, courage, and perseverance. Such as accomplished this were regarded as fit custodians of the spiritual secrets of life.

How few modern seekers could cheerfully undergo such trials! All too many who claim to be "highly advanced" are incapable of surmounting the slightest obstacle or facing with equanimity the least discomfiture or disappointment. Utterly lacking the stuff of which greatness is made, these persons look forward to speedy enlightenment, or even affirm that they are already of the body of the elect. We must agree with the elemental whom Shakespeare makes to say, "What fools these mortals be!"

It is true that the old temples with their subterranean horrors are gone, but new temples have arisen just as vast, in many ways just as great, and certainly fully as horrible. While life itself goes on, the Mystery School will continue, but the method by which candidates for spiritual enlightenment will be tested differ with each civilization and are modified to meet the needs of every age. About us now rises a great and mysterious structure; we can call it the Temple of Civilization. Civilization, like all sacred structures, was built up by men in service to an ideal, or possibly more correctly, in bondage to an idea. Our world rises up about us, a gloomy mystery of labyrinthine involvements. Like the Mystery temple, there are beautiful rooms above and terrible dungeons beneath. Its outer parts are gilded and adorned according to our noblest manner, but its foundations are being eaten away by dark creatures of the earth and by the evils men have cultivated in their quest for profits. Here is the new temple of initiation, where every day souls are tested as to their greatness and integrity, and where the gods of tomorrow are fighting the wild beasts of today's injustice and perversion. The new ritual is fitted for the new age.

No circumambulating priests with lighted tapers, no invisible voices chanting hymns to strange gods, no glory, no jeweled crowns and pleated robes; not much left in romance but an abundance of facts in the temple of modern initiation. The ladder still leads upward to the stars; man can still achieve his immortality; but the artistry and picturesqueness of the ancient religions have gone. Then, alas, we make a most unhappy discovery. W find that men are so interested in robes, crowns, and processionals that they practically refuse to be good without them. Some even confess that it was the pomp and not the virtue in which they were interested all the time, and that they see no great reason for inconveniencing themselves unless they be rewarded with a good measure of applause. Possibly men can fight tangible adversaries in the dark better than they can oppose intangible ones in the daylight; but the fact remains that many who would go out and slay lions for the glory of God—and their own as well—will not be honest, generous, or forgiving in their daily community existence.

At the present time, we are living surrounded by karmic circumstances that we have created by our own actions, and from which we are supposed to receive a liberal education and an education in liberality. A Tower of Babel built by greed and held together by crime, is perilously near a collapse. The heyday of ulterior motive is here as far as our civilization is concerned, and unless we make drastic efforts to correct the present evils, our days are numbered. The depression is the direct result of human selfishness as expressed through speculation, graft, and fictitious values, abetted by many lesser ills. At this time, those who believe that, through study and thought, they have come to a little better understanding of the laws governing life, are faced with an opportunity to prove their intelligence by meeting the present condition in a truly philosophic spirit. Here is a great initiation, one of the greatest that the chemistries of life have ever precipitated. There must be a division of civilization. That part which has courage, integrity, and vision will go on to become the forerunners of a new race; the rest will vanish as have the races that went before. Can the philosophically minded individual take the present conditions and use them as opportunities for growth and rational achievement? The test of philosophy is its sufficiency in time of adversity; for to those who actually possess spiritual insight, there is an ever-present contentment and realization of Good that is utterly independent of possession. A neophyte in the modern Mystery School is armed with the short sword of a little wisdom and launched into the darkness of an irrational world to fight the instincts of possession and selfishness. Having overcome these, the candidate has passed a real initiation test just as surely as those in the caverns of the Mithraic Mystery. Never has there been greater incentive to a betterment of the general condition, and those who meet the present crisis according to the highest standards they know, must be the forerunners and pioneers of a better order of things to come upon the earth.

*QUESTION—What is illumination?*

*Answer*—Illumination, according to the definition of mysticism, is inward enlightenment. Truth is light—not physical light, but soul light. As plants in the field grow up through the earth to the light of the sun, so man grows up through the dark earth of nature to the light of truth. Illumination may be either rational or intuitional. In the first, man discovers through reason his participation in the life of all things. He moves from reason to realization. In the second, emotion, refined and spiritualized, acts as an occult sympathy, with the result that the soul *feels* Reality. Emotional conviction raises the consciousness by enthusiasm to the Real. The end achieved in both cases is the same, but one is an occult and the other a mystical approach.

Illumination is not the end of growth; it is really man's first awareness that he is a growing part of a growing whole. Through the study of books, man gains an intellectual acceptance of the great laws of life. But when he examines himself, he realizes that he does not know that these laws are true. He only thinks they are true. He may live up to his standard of thinking, and must live up to it if his mental conviction is to be perfected by spiritual realization. Illumination is the proving of that which is believed. The inward perceptions perceive actually that which the mind has accepted because of logic or consistency. This change produces a tremendous influence in the individual. Fact, being within, produces strength and security. Weakness disappears from the soul, and man is positive and the world becomes negative. Instead of man being a small uncertainty in a great certainty, man himself becomes certain. The increased strength and dedication make possible the higher steps of evolution that lie beyond.

Illumination should not be regarded as the end of the mystical life, but rather the true beginning of it. A person is not perfect because he is illumined, but rather is one step closer to perfection because of the establishment of a new and higher standard of understanding. Illumination should never be regarded as a solution to personal problems in the sense that it brings with it any improvement of the temporal state. Illumination does not confer health, happiness, and prosperity in material matters. It confers the ability to understand more clearly the reason why things happen. It increases patience, deepens appreciation, and strengthens the virtues. Illumination also brings a measure of detachment from material overemphasis. It does not decrease the difficulties of living, but gives greater strength to overcome these difficulties.

There are many degrees of illumination. The small boy in school is illumined by the increase of his knowledge. The disciple, seeing spiritual things for the first time, is illumined by the extension of his horizon. The great adept who unfolds, in rising from one exalted state to another, is also illumined by the new experiences of this growth. Illumination, like life, is a perpetual unfoldment, but the term is most often used to signify man's first flash of the Eternal.

*QUESTION—What is cosmic consciousness?*

*Answer*—The term *cosmic consciousness* literally means the consciousness of the cosmos, or the consciousness that ensouls the cosmos. Cosmic consciousness is therefore the pattern-binder, the realization of wholeness, by which all the elements of the universe are bound into a cosmic unity. Only the cosmos can know the cosmos, for in this case, knowing is not the product of thinking. Knowing is an attribute of being, and wholeness ensouls the whole.

A certain type of metaphysician talks glibly about cosmic consciousness. He may refer to his own consciousness as being cosmic or one with the cosmos. But unfortunately, while man remains man, he is not cosmic; when he becomes cosmic, he is no longer man. Between the human being and cosmic consciousness is the whole interval of magnitudes and multitudes that divides the human being from the cosmos. Inconceivable aeons of time must pass before man can unfold a cosmos from within himself and ensoul it with his realization. If a student cannot understand his brother who is similar to himself, how can he understand the cosmos which contains the similitudes of all things? The particular can never grasp the universal, and only ages of universalization can bring to man the capacity to mingle his own personal attitudes with the streams of purposes which make up life.

What metaphysicians mean by cosmic consciousness, referring to their own experiences, is an extension of consciousness. Such an extension brings with it a certain measure of understanding concerning matters not previously understood, a certain measure of realization concerning matters not previously realized. Perceiving a little more, man mistakes the little for the All; being a little wiser, he mistakes a little wisdom for All Wisdom, exaggerating the significance of his experience.

It may be that through long studies, a devout person may suddenly awake to the realization of the universality of God or the fundamental identity of life. These discoveries, flowing in upon the mind, overwhelm the intellect with their magnitude and significance. Seeing values for the first time, and lifted to a high state of exaltation, a little improvment assumes the proportion of ultimates. Perspective is lost in an overwhelming experience. The student does not realize that he is only at the beginning of understanding. He has forgotten that even the gods grow. No matter how deep and sincere our consciousness may be, perfection is not yet. It is one extension of realization to understand that the cosmos *is consciousness,* but it is a still more advanced state of realization to achieve identity with the consciousness of the cosmos. The first is possible to man, the second is remote even to the gods.

*QUESTION—How do you reconcile the Eastern teaching of non-action and the Western teaching of service to humanity?*

*Answer—*The difficulty here is due to a misunderstanding of the term *non-action.* Eastern schools do not preach inertia, but rather that the wise man performs no action that is not true, beautiful, and necessary. The Oriental philosopher is more of a realist in many ways than is the Occidental thinker. The cultural experience of thousands of years has taught Asia lessons that the West has yet to learn. The East realizes that most action is unneccesary and unimportant. To strive after things is vanity, to desire things is folly, and to think that you can help others is excessive optimism. For these reasons, the Oriental sage leans on his forked stick and lets the world go by, realizing that no matter what we may try to do, it will still go by, and the man does not live who can save ignorannt human beings from the rewards of their own stupidity.

The Easterner is fundamentally a fatalist. He is not cynical nor unsympathetic, nor inhuman, but experience has taught him that each individual must live his own life and find truth in his own way. So as the sage sits by the road, it may occur that some one of the passers-by may turn off and come to him. This is also fatalism to the Eastern mind, for those who are ready will seek for those who know, and there is no need for wise men to cry their wares. When the disciple finds his guru, the master gives him no encouragement. Those who are ready for knowledge need no encouragement, and all the encouragement in the world is useless to those who are not ready.

Nor does the Eastern sage normally concern himself with matters outside his own intellectual province. It is the duty of a physician to heal the sick, of farmers to till the ground, of shop-keepers to buy and sell, of priests to dust off the altars, and of pundits to teach. It is the sage's duty to perform that labor which no other man can perform—the instruction of the soul. Farmers cannot do the work of philosophers, nor should philosophers do the work of farmers. Each on his own plane or level, should perform the work suitable to himself, and it is the duty of the philosopher to wait, wait longer, and then wait some more. When he has waited long enough, those who need that which he alone can give will struggle their way to him.

Certain of this, the Asiatic mystic meditates through the years, oblivious to the change of empire about him. Nations may rise and fall, wars and pestilences may come and go, but in every age and under all conditions, there will be some who will need wisdom, will appreciate it and know how to use it. So the mystic waits, realizing that, as Walt Whitman said, that which is his own shall know his face.

But the Westerner has a different attitude. His religions have extolled the virtues of charity, humanitarianism, and service to mankind. The Western mystic believes that in feeding the hungry, clothing the naked, and ministering to the physical needs of the indigent, he is living up to the highest standards of his faith. There can be no doubt that this attitude has made life easier for thousands of people, and we highly honor in this Western world those who dedicate themselves and their means to the alleviation of human suffering and human want. More than this, we look forward to a time when new economics and social adjustment will bring economic security to all.

The Western religions have the strongest social vision, and this has resulted in a far better material state than that enjoyed by Eastern peoples. Nor would it be right to deny that good motive frequently inspires the Westerner's altruism. He believes in being a good Samaritan, he believes in helping all who need, and his purse is always open in time of distress or crisis.

The term *Christian charity* is frequently used to describe the financial generosity of the Occidental. Democracy contributes also to this viewpoint. Jesus affirmed universal brotherhood, and his inferences were definitely democratic. The Occidental has elevated the concept of democracy to the dignity of religion, and, firmly of the belief that he is able to legislate the equality of man, he is convinced that he is contributing to the permanent betterment of the whole human race.

Western religion has no esoteric schools to direct the religious aspirations of the laity. The obscuration of the secret doctrine has left action as the only means of applying spiritual ideals. Men and women who ought to be hard at work studying the laws of nature are reduced to performing those "little acts of kindness" which, though perfectly good in themselves, are not the real ultimate of religion.

Yet those long experienced in "little acts of kindness" find that helping people is the most difficult thing in the world.

A wealthy man with a fortune to give away can only pray to all-wise Providence that his generosity will not do more harm than good. The philanthropist has extraordinary experiences. In trying to lift men up, he usually only casts them down. The more he does, the more he can do, and he often finds an ungrateful world that sops up his charity, and makes bad karma for himself in the process. Charity obscures the working of the law of cause and effect, a thing in itself dangerous, and when a whole civilization develops humanitarianism without depth of understanding, the result is demoralizing to the integrity of the masses. A man who has any reason to believe that he can enjoy the securities of life as the result of the benevolence of others rapidly loses interest in improving himself.

Possibly the best examples of service without understanding are charitable institutions. No one can deny that while they exist, and while society makes them necessary, they must be supported, but it is a strange thing that the Christian charity that takes care of the helpless did not assert itself in preventing it rather than in curing it. Under our present system of civilization, charitable institutions are absolute proofs of the lack of Christianity or any other religious principle in the economic and social fabric. The forethought comes behind.

Rich men trying to give away money have realized the fallacy of passing it on to individuals. The result is that vast conscience-funds are being turned over to educational and scientific institutions to be used to increase the horizon of the young or improve the health of the aged. But here again, the charity is blocked. Education and science lack the perspective themselves to consider any of man's needs above the purely physical and economic. The richest nation in the world suddenly discovers that there is nothing important that money can buy. Charity comes to nothing, because nothing you can give an individual can make him truly happy, truly safe, or truly wise. We can take care of the hunger in his body, but the hunger in his soul is beyond our capacity to feed.

Service is therefore limited by lack of religious understanding. We can only do the thing that we know to do, and we know so very little about life and law and love that we are poor guardians over these natural truths, and worse administrators. We mean well, but we have ignored philosophy so long that we really do not know what we mean. We try, but the trial and error system seems productive mostly of error. It may dawn upon the Western world sometime that there is definite need in its world for that inner sufficiency which is embodied in the Oriental philosopher leaning on his forked stick under some banana palm. He knows much, and sits still; we know little, and run around unceasingly. We are trying to do good, but he is the one who knows what good is. Is it not also possible that the inaction of the Eastern sage has so compelling a force about it that in the end the Western world will make a pilgrimage to his feet? If and when this occurs, the truth will be apparent that his silent meditation was more powerful, more significant, and more enduring than all the institutions we have built in the desperate effort to change the fundamentals of human nature by outward means.

# HEALTH AND THE LAWS OF
# PHYSICAL LIFE

## PART SEVEN

*QUESTION—What are the laws of health?*

*Answer*—Health is normalcy, and all that promotes normalcy promotes health. The Classical philosophers define health as the natural state of man, viewing sickness and disease as the result of ignorance and intemperance. Health is not merely physical integrity; it is the harmony of the inner life manifesting through the physical organism. Most of the ills of the flesh can be traced to wrong thinking and undisciplined emotion. It would not be right, however, to teach that health can be achieved through inhibiting and repressing. It would be more correct to say that health can be achieved by intelligent direction, in which the energies of life are directed into channels of constructive and appropriate expression.

Every normal human being desires to express himself, and in every life there are secret hopes and aspirations. To choose some constructive and worthy aim, and to live toward it, dedicating the life and thought toward accomplishment, is to find happiness and usually a higher degree of physical health. Purposeless people are sick with and of themselves. People struggling after unworthy ambitions, are diseased by the falseness of their purpose, and people living down to a code unworthy of them are disintegrating themselves by retro-

191

gressive feeling and thinking. A few simple rules may help the metaphysician to live up to the standards which he himself has recognized as suitable and consistent.

1.  Preserve the normalcy of the body by obeying the rudimentary laws of health—sanitation, exercise, ventilation, and healthful environment.

2. Preserve the functions of the body through reasonable methods of eating, with especial attention to the problem of elimination.

3. Normalize relationships with environment and other people. If it is impossible to be where we desire to be, and among people we desire to know, the individual must rise above his natural tendency to dissatisfaction and accomplish serenity where he is, among the people with whom he is associated.

4. Every effort should be made to refine and beautify the emotions and feelings. Grief, hate, jealousy, envy, self-pity, and all the morbid, hysterical emotions must be redirected if anything resembling normal health is to be expected. Usually emotions can find constructive and natural expression through esthetics, or one of the arts, or good, constructive and strenuous work.

5. Irrationalities of the mind must also be tempered with moderation. Lives filled with schemes, excuses, and melancholies contribute little to security. Worries, griefs, and morbid anticipations bring about a fulfillment of themselves at the expense of the health.

6. Complexes and fixations arising in the subconscious mind must also be worked with and overcome. Habits, easy through long usage, must often be corrected. Nearly every person carries throughout life irascibilities that are termed temperament, which he believes cannot be overcome. Every-

thing can be overcome, but it may require considerable effort over a long period of time. A person who desires to be well must conquer the tendencies in his living which destroy health.

Health is that which remains when the stupidities of man have been removed by intelligent effort. The human being cannot create health, or force a condition of physical well-being. Health is one of the results of wisdom, and only the wise can be truly well.

*QUESTION—What do you advise on the subject of diet?*

*Answer*—It appears in practice that extreme attitudes toward food are productive of dyspepsia rather than health. A few simple rules may suggest a wise and balanced approach:

1. Eat *moderately,* remembering that most foods are digestible in reasonable quantities, and the amount eaten is more likely to cause trouble than any particular food product.

2. Eat according to the work you are doing, emphasizing such food products as are known to provide the type of energy suited to your occupation or profession.

3. Eat a moderate *variety* of foods, but do not mix incompatible elements in any single meal.

4. Unless you are suffering from some particular disease aggravated by certain kinds of foods, eat moderately of what you *like,* for miserable and unattractive combinations are seldom beneficial.

5. Try to eat *regularly.* If your present eating does not seem satisfactory, try increasing the number of meals and decreasing the amount of food eaten at each. Herbivorous animals in particular nibble most of the time, and if it produces contented cows, it may have unsuspected virtues for

mankind. This formula is of special value to people of very small appetite and anemic tendencies.

6. As important as the quality of food is its *attractiveness* of appearance and the environment in which it is eaten. The proper digestion of food demands that the system develop a pleasant anticipation, and the eyes are ministers to the gastric juices.

7. *Simple foods,* not highly seasoned, are usually the most healthful and, to those of normal appetite, the most welcome. The modern tendency to complicate cuisine and to have a large number of courses to the meal works hardship upon the digestive processes. One of the ancient laws of health was that a person living in a community should eat the foods of his community and should vary his menu with the seasons, eating at each season the foods natural to that season, thus equipping the body to meet the external factors of climate and temperature.

8. We hear a great deal of talk about getting back to natural foods, but it should be remembered that man has been away from primitive spinach and raw meat for many thousands of years, and to suddenly adjust a system that has been reared on artificial foods to some hearty Pliocene eating, often proves disastrous. The body adjusts slowly, and having come to some particular rhythm, resists efforts to change its function. It should be worked with carefully and patiently.

9. The philosopher is not generally one of those food-conscious individuals who is constantly worrying about his calories, his carbohydrates, or his vitamins. He realizes that it is not the duty of the evolved human being to keep his mind forever on his stomach, wasting years of thinking on the mere simple process of feeding himself. Choose a simple,

reasonable, and pleasant diet, and free the intellect to work on the great problems of the hour.

10. If it be true that a man digs his grave with his teeth, it is equally true that most mortals worry, fear, and plague themselves into an early grave wrestling with problems of small merit and consequence.

From the earliest times, religious institutions have regarded diet as an important aspect of spiritual culture. The systems of eating recommended by these various groups differ in some ways, but for the most part agree on the essential principles. All religious and philosophical schools have warned against over-eating as the worst of dietetic evils. Too much food, and elaborate and complicated menus, receive the weight of general censure. The Pythagoreans advised moderation and simplicity, and the followers of the school enjoyed extraordinary health and longevity. According to the tradition, Pythagoras himself, when nearly 100 years of age, had the strength and endurance of a youth in his twenties. Apollonius of Tyana, who followed the Pythagorean disciplines, was physically and mentally in his prime at the age of 100.

A reasonable viewpoint on this subject for modern consideration would emphasize the evil of excess, with one reservation. Diets for the philosophically minded should not be imposed upon growing children who require much more of food than persons of mature years. Over-feeding after middle life is particularly unfortunate, and it has been scientifically proved that the body survives longer on hunger than it does on satiety. The wise course is to discover the minimum upon which the body flourishes and adhere to it.

As to the nature of that which is to be eaten, there is less uniformity of belief. Various races have food staples that are accepted as indispensable, but again, there is agreement that foods which undergo elaborate processes of refinement or cooking are to be avoided. Most religious diets work for energy-building foods with low starch content. Pythagoras advised grain, cheese, fruit, and vegetables that mature above the ground; nor does he seem to have condemned the eating of meat. But he advised magistrates to refrain from eating meat for twenty-four hours previous to decisions in court, for the sake of mental clarity.

Generally speaking, a moderate, well-balanced meal of natural foods is suitable for general use, but no elaborate departure should be made from eating habits without the assistance of a skilled dietician. The various abnormalities of body chemistry, present in nearly every person living in our peculiar social system, should never be overlooked when planning a diet. Extensive fasting was discouraged among the more philosophic sects, although the entirely devout frequently starved themselves to death. If the amount of food necessary to the bodily economy is skillfully gauged, there is no need for fasting to clean out the system.

Some of the old schools taught that the clarity of the reason was improved by abstaining from food one day each week, and eating a normal amount the rest of the time. The Mohammedan fast of Ramadan was instituted as a physical aid to the spiritual life, due to the rather intemperate eating of the Moslem world. There is no food panacea for the evils of the soul. No man shall reach heaven by dieting alone. The ability of the human being to function at a maximum of efficiency demands the proper fueling for his physical engine.

It has generally been observed that if a person interested in metaphysical matters uses a general moderation in his eating, the law of natural selection will gradually assert itself. A person doing intensive mental work will naturally rebel against the sluggishness caused by the over-eating of coarse, low-vibration foods. The diet will be corrected by the inward tendencies of the mind and life. Occasionally, we meet a person who regards himself as a very advanced metaphysician, who at the same time is wrestling with the diet demon. The fact is that no one highly advanced in metaphysical matters will have any such conflict. The diet will be determined not by the appetites, but by the chemistry that philosophy has set up in the bodily organisms.

Do not steel yourself against eating things you believe are inconsistent with philosophy; rather, perfect the philosophy and you will find that natural selection will cause you to finally eat that which is useful to you. In the average person, unfortunately, the law of natural selection is obscured by the artificiality of the conditions under which we live. As Socrates so wisely observed: "Moderation is the cornerstone of the virtues." Nor should we forget the entirely significant words of the Nazarene teacher: "It is not that which goeth in at the mouth that defileth a man; it is that which cometh out of the mouth that defileth a man."

*QUESTION—Do you recommend fasting as a means of advancing spiritually?*

*Answer*—According to the opinion of H. G. Wells, Gautama Buddha was one of the three greatest men who ever lived upon the earth. Buddha's experience in fasting therefore should be of interest and significance to all students of philosophy. When Buddha set forth on his quest for enlightenment, he followed the Brahman discipline of his time, giving himself over to extreme austerities of the flesh. He performed elaborate fastings for the purification of his soul until, at last, weakened from starvation, he sank down exhausted by the side of the Indian road. His years of self-sacrifice and suffering had failed utterly to bring him the illumination that he sought. Realizing his failure, Buddha ate a hearty meal, and gave up the penitent path of starvation. It was only after he had restored the health and normalcy of his physical body that illumination came to him.

It is true that fasting will stimulate the psychical powers by breaking down body resistance, but the way of true wisdom is not through psychism, but through the normalizing and perfecting of every part of the nature. In matters of food, the Socratic axiom is admirable: "In all things not too much." Moderation, and not abstinence, is normalcy. The theory of starving to death for the glory of God belongs to the old era of superstitions. The philosopher of today realizes that the law of life is not fulfilled through misery and suffering, but that the universal plan is perfected by the health, happiness, and well-being of all creatures.

*QUESTION—Do parents give their progeny only physical bodies?*

*Answer*—The old wisdom teachings reject what is commonly known as the law of heredity, explaining that the phenomonen generally ascribed to heredity has its real source in reincarnation and karma. By the law of attraction, the ego at birth is drawn into an environment similar to itself and suitable for the working out of its karma. Thus an entity whose karma it is to suffer the experience of tuberculosis, will be drawn into a tubercular family where it will receive a body susceptible to this disease. Science says that we do not inherit disease, but tendency to disease. Thus parental environment and physical heredity are the instruments of the universal justice. Children resemble their parents in temperament because entities of similar temperaments incarnate in similar families and environments, by the natural law that like attracts like.

*QUESTION—What should be the attitude of the occult student toward surgery?*

*Answer*—Persons of all beliefs approach surgery with a common dread. The intelligence of the individual warns him that the human body is an extremely delicate mechanism, which seldom fully recovers from major surgery. The physical man is a masterpiece of natural economy. All the organs and parts of the body have a particular duty to perform, and removal of any organ or part is bound to influence the vibratory and chemical balance of the whole structure.

Several ancient peoples, most notably the Greeks, held all surgery and dissection in disfavor, declaring it to be a sacrilege against the gods and the human soul to mutilate its house either in life or after death. It is for this reason that the Greeks never achieved any high proficiency in anatomy but did accomplish much in clinical medicine. The clinics of Hippocrates contained hundreds of patients under constant observation, but the physicians gathered there possessed only the most rudimentary knowledge of the organs of the body, their location, and general structure.

Of late years, surgery has become more or less of a medical fad, and prominent surgeons have grown wealthy from the exorbitant fees they charge for even the most minor operations. The average sick person, having little knowledge of his own functions, is intimidated into surgery through high-pressure business methods. On the other hand, there are many people living lives of comparative comfort and efficiency who would be dead had not surgery rescued them from some physical extremity.

Philosophically speaking, it seems to me that the matter can be summarized something like this: the purpose of life is experience. Under normal conditions, the perpetuation of life offers opportunity for growth and usefulness. It is the duty of the individual, therefore, to perpetuate life as long as there is any reasonable probability of the restoration of comparative health. To fail in this respect, and perhaps to die rather than to use the scientific means available to prolong life, would not be regarded as a philosophical virtue, but is, technically speaking, suicide. Philosophy will therefore permit the use of surgery when other means have failed and surgery is the last recourse. Philosophy would invite each truth seeker to live as nearly as possible in harmony with the laws of health, but in an emergency, would regard the perpetuation of life as more important than anti-surgery prejudices.

*QUESTION—What is your advice in the matters of eugenics and birth control?*

*Answer*—In past centuries it was the opinion of good orthodox people that children were the gift of divine providence, and that the largeness or smallness of a family depended entirely on celestial and theological factors. Also, less strenuous economic periods, with agriculture as the principal element in the economic system, favored large families and insured reasonable opportunities of health and usefulness. Most ancient nations valued the institution of the home, honored parenthood, and encouraged early marriages and numerous offspring.

Conditions have considerably changed. The human soul is faced with a new cycle of experiences. The home has broken down. Human relationships are particularly insecure, and parents are ever less willing to sacrifice their own interests for the arduous and uncertain task of rearing families. Also, there is a realization arising in a considerable bloc of the public mind that there are enough people in the world; in fact, so many that half of the living are starving to death. Society is now bringing to bear an innumerable array of influences to discourage large families, which increase the hazards of child rearing.

In substance, the difficulties are as follows: the heavy cost of bringing children into the world, the prohibitive cost of educating them, and the prohibitive cost of giving them a reasonable place in the social system. It has been estimated that the average child costs ten thousand dollars to bring to the age of majority, with what may be termed the proper advantages of his day. This is many years' salary for the average working man; not only years of work, but years of worry and anxiety, self-denial and sacrifice. And after all this has been accomplished, the young hopeful may be drafted into an army and be one of those thousands who die at dawn and lie in unmarked graves.

As man thinks things through, as science and philosophy instruct him in life's probabilities, he cannot be entirely blamed if his optimism fails in the presence of a wide array of discouraging facts. The whole matter is well shown in the young people growing up through the depression. Many of them want to be married, establish homes, and raise families, but the money hazards render these normal impulses not only impractical, but impossible. The world conspires against the individual, apparently doing everything possible to make life difficult and hazardous. A society that cannot protect life, offers small incentive for families and family sentiments.

Another important element is the increasing moronity and criminal degeneracy that result from man's inhumanity to man. It has been estimated that one out of five of the population must be considered as subnormal, and the number of criminals in America alone is simply unbelievable, actually running into the millions. When underprivileged people marry, their limitations are stamped upon their progeny, creating more and more problems for society to solve.

It has been advanced that the sterilization of the unfit would be a major step forward in coping with degeneracy and disease. From an occult standpoint, I cannot see that this would violate any fundamental law. In the first place, it would improve the general tone of society, giving a better grade of entities opportunities to incarnate; and in the second place, it would not limit the incarnation of lower grades of entities, since there are innumerable divisions among the lower brackets of civilization for the incoming of less evolved types. Actually, degeneracy is not natural. That which is natural is right, and it is natural that man, coming into incarnation, should find a reasonably healthy vehicle for his manifestation. The karma that he causes by functioning through an inappropriate body could be prevented if he had a better vehicle to work with, a better environment to grow up in, and a better world to live in. According to Buddhism, a cause, once set in motion, must produce an effect. But if the cause is prevented, the effect is also prevented.

At the present time, large families are principally limited to the lower classes of society. The large families of the poor are proverbial, and the charitable resources of the community are taxed to the breaking point by the biological optimism of the impoverished. Considerable religious prejudice still contributes to this unfair and unreasonable state of things. It would be far better to bring up one or two children in reasonable security than to attempt the almost impossible task of raising a dozen in a condition of mutual malnutrition. Law must take the place of philosophy until the individual achieves to common sense in his own life. A wider teaching of the principles of eugenics and birth control, particularly among poorer people of society, could only result in better homes and better advantages for both parents and children.

While it is true that the perpetuation of the race depends upon the home and family, it is also true that man, having risen above the animal in many other things, is not merely a breeder. Family relationships have been elevated above animal standards of breeding, and it is proper that philosophy, esthetics, and culture should flourish together in the life of man, and should refine all his physical processes.

*QUESTION—What is spiritual or faith healing, and is it ethical?*

*Answer*—The use of superphysical forces, or of superphysical means to restore the physical health of the body is properly called spiritual or faith healing. There are several forms of metaphysical healing: by prayer, by suggestion, by magnetism or hypnosis, or by individual or collective concentrated thought directed to the patient. There are also forms of spiritual healing making use of decarnate entities, elementals, and on rare occasions the control and direction of the subtle forces of nature by initiates and adepts.

Metaphysical healing derives its authority directly from divine revelation. The founders of nearly all great religious movements, with the possible exception of Mohammed, are all accredited with possessing a supernatural power. In most cases, miracles are attributed to them. What pious Christian would deny the power of faith over disease when his own Savior had raised the dead, opened the eyes of the blind, and given to his disciples power to heal the sick in his name? The problem of miracles leaves materia medica and theology in a deadlock. Although the Protestant clergy did not assert its privilege of treating disease by virtue of the admonition of its founder, it was certainly sympathetic to the idea that God could bestow at his pleasure a curative virtue upon individuals untrained in medical science. Many of our medical specialists disagree on this, but must state their opinions in a modulated voice, lest they lose patients.

When the student of philosophy exchanges the fallacies of theology for the ordered life of the wise, he is apt to find himself upon the horns of a dilemma. He learns that the universe is controlled by Law—absolute and immutable. Realizing the world to be no respecter of persons, and himself to be surrounded by principles of such cosmic magnitude that he is scarcely an equation in their activity, he may be excused if at first he verges unduly toward fatalism.

A fatalistic attitude has a tendency to dilute the milk of human kindness. For if an individual is in the place that he has earned for himself—as philosophy certainly affirms— and is surrounded by experiences necessary to the development of his character, should another turn from his own pursuits and interfere with the laws of destiny by helping this fellow creature over a rough spot in the road of life? In fact, is it really possible to save a person from an experience through which fate has decreed that he should pass? The law of compensation, or karma, which is simply the principle of cause and effect applied to the individualized destinies of men, decrees that as we sow, so shall we reap. It is difficult for the average person to affirm this doctrine without a dulling effect upon the fine edge of sympathy, creating a sense of hopelessness in the face of a dominating providence.

Theologies are more or less emotional revolts against the exactness of philosophic law. People like to believe that they can escape consequences by the patented processes of the clergy. To the theologically minded, the fine points of philosophy are of no great consequence, for they can explain themselves both out of hell and into heaven, and through all sorts of temporal dilemmas, with amazing ease. The individual, weighing the apparent contradictions and desiring to hew as closely as possible to the line of right, is most sorely perplexed. Such questions as these are often asked: Does a physician who cures some disorder of the flesh oppose the law of nature and commit a grievous wrong? Should we try to heal others of their affliction, or should we leave them to their own resources? Is it permissible for us to save a life when, without our intervention, it would certainly be lost? Is magnetic healing black magic? Is hypnotism ever justifiable? Should spiritual forces be used in an effort to correct physical ills?

To clarify these matters, let us first of all try to understand the nature or substance of disease. Buddha says that all the evils to which the flesh is heir have their common origin in ignorance. Ignorance is almost synonymous with unbalance, for wisdom and equilibrium are certainly closely related terms. Disease is an unnatural state to a creature living a natural existence, and being inconsistent with the latter state, does not manifest there. To creatures who live unnaturally and surround themselves with artificial circumstances, disease is natural, for cause and effect decrees that normalcy shall generate normalcy and abnormality produce its kind. Hence all disease is seated in some shortcoming that opens the individual to such afflictions.

The illnesses that may afflict mankind can exist on any of three planes—mental, emotional, and physical—and through the afflictions set up on one of these planes, the rest of the nature may be infested so that finally the whole structure collapses. When we speak of mental disease, we do not necessarily mean insanity, but any excess of thought for scheming and plotting and deceit; in fact, the holding of any unkind or destructive attitude is sufficient to disease the whole organism and wrack the body with a score of pains. By emotional diseases we mean to imply any excess, as of hate, jealousy or even such apparently worthy emotions as piety and affection, for these, if pushed to the point of a vice, are as dangerous as anger or lust. Physical diseases are too numerous and well known to need description. They are a diversified host of ills, a great percentage of which are traceable to a mental or emotional source. Only a small percentage belongs definitely to the intemperances of the flesh.

According to philosophy, a physician is capable of treating a disease for one of two definite ends: first, to achieve a complete cure; second, to effect a temporary healing in which the patient is released from an imminent crisis, but must ultimately face the situation again. The occult physician knows that to accomplish a complete cure, he must stamp out the intemperance at its root; he must find the source of the condition, and work the problem out on its own plane of activity. If the trouble is referable to some idiosyncracy, there is no use giving pills; the condition must be worked out upon the mental plane. If an emotional excess is the cause of the disorder, then upon the emotional plane must the correction be made. Again, physical ailments must be treated with physical remedies. Of course the physician cannot hope to effect a complete cure without the intelligent cooperation of the patient. By correcting the excesses which the wise physician has diagnosed as responsible for the ailment, the matter is entirely cleared up, for the cause, being removed, can no longer generate effects. No one can expect to be well who has unnatural attitudes, feelings, or appetites. This both the physician and the patient must realize.

The healer will not go far astray if he makes it his unalterable rule to work out his patient's problems with the means common to the plane upon which those problems exist. For instance, if the seat of the disorder is diagnosed as purely physical, use natural physical means to correct the condition. In other words, if it is discovered that the patient has a vertebra out of place, the course to be pursued is evident. Do not sit around affirming that the vertebra is back in its natural position or engage a spiritual healer to give treatments, absent or otherwise. Do not "hold the thought" and pray for an invisible adept or try to enlist the services of an archangel—go to a good osteopath and have it put back, in this way greatly conserving the spiritual resources of the universe!

Spiritual forces should be used for spiritual problems, mental forces for mental problems, emotional forces for emotional problems, and physical forces for physical problems. To divert a force to some illegitimate end is equivalent to sorcery. What the herbs of the fields are to the body, beauty is to the emotions, and rationality to the mind. To divert mental forces to the achievement of physical ends is a perversion of power, for it binds the greater to the lesser. The mind, for example, is unquestionably capable of controlling the body, and by virtue of that sovereignty, can mold the body into its purposes. You can stop pain by mental power, and every day we hear of wonderful results obtained by mental healing. But in the process, a sacred treaty between the parts of man has been violated. Force—not reason—has accomplished the result. The demands of the body have not been met; mind has ridden roughshod over the laws of matter. Black magic must be the term applied where might instead of right achieves desired ends.

It often occurs that the physician is brought into the presence of a critical state in which the cooperation of the patient cannot be expected. The laws of mercy demand an immediate action. Under such conditions, a cure is not the object, for a cure is impossible until the patient can cure himself. The physician can only direct. The main purpose is to assist the sufferer over the immediate condition, in order that he may be given an opportunity to work out his problem under less acute circumstances. If the patient should die of the disease, he must reincarnate again and thus create a new opportunity to work out the problem. The physician who can preserve the life of his patient and give him an earlier opportunity to cope with his extremity, thus contributes to the economy of nature. Technically, a physician cannot interfere with karma; he can only delay its processes.

Considering the employment of hypnosis, we will suppose that an individual is suffering from a drug habit (hypnosis being used particularly in the treatment of this as well as other undesirable habits). As the result of hypnosis, the patient loses all interest in narcotics and lives the life of a peaceful and useful citizen. Philosophy teaches that this person has not actually escaped from the drug habit; he has only been given a respite, but the problem is presented to him again, possibly in a different way, until the weakness of that particular tendency is overcome. Much good has been accomplished, however, for a long chain of potential bad karma has been prevented. If the habit had not been cured, a great deal more bad karma would have been generated. The habit might have led to excess and even to crime, for evils multiply more rapidly than the proverbial guinea pigs. Philosophy teaches that while we cannot escape such karma as we have already earned for ourselves, we can stop making new karma that will overshadow the future. We have no right to interfere with the workings of the law, but, as the Buddha so beautifully taught, we are privileged to free ourselves from unpleasant reactions by becoming too wise to do those things which cause suffering. We are privileged to assist others in this respect also. Hypnosis should never be regarded as a cure, and occultism in no way advocates its promiscuous use. In fact, occult science discourages all metaphysical processes, reserving such for conditions where every single natural method has failed.

Every physician who uses spiritual methods of healing should unfailingly warn his patient that such methods are in no sense substitutes for the correction of the cause of the ailment. The healer should explain the principles of natural and normal living, and demand intelligent cooperation on the part of the sufferer. In recent years, metaphysical healing has become a popular substitute for individual integrity. The healer has taken the place of the priest who once served out "redemption through grace." To benumb one's sense of individual responsibility and depend upon some spiritual healer for health, happiness, and normalcy is to court inevitable disaster. Such things cannot be. A healer is not greater than the Law, and while he may be sufficiently gifted to produce extraordinary results, nature inevitably reasserts itself and only that which is real will survive.

The gods revealed the art of healing at the very beginning of civilization. Humanity, incapable of applying all the principles of health, hobbles along with the aid of a crutch for lack of which it might otherwise fall by the way. Crutches at best are unsatisfactory, however, and true health is the only utterly desirable state. The spiritual healer who, with gentleness of spirit, offers his powers for the mending of broken lives, gives himself to a very beautiful task. But woe to the one who attempts to exert force and create desired conditions through the sheer force of will—such a person is dealing in sorcery whether the actual purposes are malevolent or benevolent. The healer must take the attitude of impelling but never compelling any conditions that he desires to bring about. It is wise for him always to keep in mind that not his will, but the greatest ultimate good, must be done.

*QUESTION—Why is it that child prodigies are usually "burned out" by the time they mature? Why do they not go on developing?*

*Answer*—The phenomenon we call a prodigy, in most cases, is the result of an imbalance of the endocrine system. The pineal gland controls the flow of mental energy from the ego to the brain, and improper function of this gland may produce the appearance of premature development and maturity. Usually, however, the physical body is incapable of sustaining the strain of premature activity, and the abnormal condition finally results in the brain or the body breaking down. Children from the fifth to fifteenth year are in the growing period. During this time, a considerable part of the vital reserve of the body must be expended in building bone, flesh, nerve, and muscle. If, during this period, glandular imbalance throws a heavy mental or emotional strain upon the body, the vital resources are divided. This results in the final weakening of both the mental and physical processes. Most parents think children are clever if they seem old beyond their years, but the efficiency of the mature individual depends to a great measure upon the normalcy of the childhood and adolescent periods.

*QUESTION—What effect has the use of medicinal drugs on the physical body, the inner bodies and centers, and the evolution of the ego?*

*Answer*—Nearly all narcotic drugs directly affect the nervous system, which is the link connecting the consciousness with the physical body. By forcing the condition of sleep, they cause the separation of the higher etheric and astral bodies from the lower etheric and dense physical form. The effect of all drugs upon the physical body is, to a certain degree, destructive. They cause a struggle in the system, in which the life within the body battles against, and finally overcomes, the foreign substances introduced. In some cases, however, they are legitimate, inasmuch as they prevent a greater struggle occurring as the result of pain or insomnia. They produce but a very slight effect in the invisible bodies, and to a slight degree slow down temporarily the whirling vortices or centers; but, of course, no physical substance is capable of injuring the ego itself other than by reflex. The only danger is the possibility of the drug causing a negative condition in the physical body, which makes the active operation of the spirit through the body difficult.

*QUESTION—Is there any virtue in sleeping with the head to the north, south, east or west?*

*Answer—*As all the occult mysteries have written, man is a miniature world, and the magnetic currents of his body correspond with the vaster currents moving about and through the earth. It would naturally follow that if man harmonizes the direction of the flow of his own energies with the flow of the energies of the earth, he will avoid conflict between his own life and the life of the world. In the northern hemisphere, it is proper to sleep with the head to the north, so that the magnetic currents flow parallel with the spine. In the southern hemisphere, the head should be to the south; and in the equatorial zone, the head should be to the east. Experimentation has proved that by following this rule, rest is more perfect, and in some cases relief has been found for restless sleeping, confused dreams, and insomnia.

It would be wrong to say that failure to follow this rule would prevent sleep or endanger the individual, but a certain added benefit results from cooperating with nature in every possible way. Of course, to sleep with one's head in the right direction does not produce spirituality. It merely increases body normalcy, in this way giving added vitality and efficiency which, through proper direction, may contribute to spiritual improvement.

*QUESTION—What is the best way to overcome an obses-
sion?*

*Answer—*The word *obsession* has two meanings at the present time. Occultly speaking, an obsession is a form of possession in which a living person is overshadowed or dominated by the intelligence of another entity. Most often the
other entity is decarnate. Psychologically speaking, an obsession is a fixation in which the natural flow of the intellect
is deflected, or perverted, by some idea or notion that has
come to dominate the reasoning processes.

In the case of true obsession, it is my observation that
certain physical derangements are usually present. Persons
of normal mental attitudes, well directed emotions, and healthy
physical bodies are seldom obsessed. Obsessions most generally
occur as the result of dabbling in occult sciences, years of emotional excess or repression, and a condition of anemia in
the body chemistry. It follows that if the obsessed person has
periods of lucidity and self-control, he should set to work
normalizing his life.

Where the obsession is continuous and the patient can
offer no personal assistance, those treating the obsession must
do everything possible to normalize the patient without his
assistance. The resistance of the physical body must be brought
up, but at the same time, it is dangerous to feed an obsessed person animal foods. Obsessing entities are usually of
a lower moral and mental caliber than the person whom they
attack, but in order for the obsession to continue, there must
be a negative link of sympathy between the entity obsessing
and the person obsessed. This link of sympathy must be
sought for and removed.

A serious case of obsession will not generally respond to
amateur treatment, but must be worked on by a person ex-

perienced in occult therapeutics. Mild cases arising from mediumship can generally be remedied by the sufferer himself if he will reorganize his spiritual life and place it on a strong individual foundation. Thought power is a great force in working with obsessions, and constructive thought regularly directed to the sufferer by a group of sympathetic people, has been known to work wonders. In no case, however, should these thought impulses be sent forth in a destructive way even against the obsessing entity, for we do not fight evil with evil, but with good.

*QUESTION—Is rejuvenation or physical immortality possible or desirable? Is it true that men should live much longer than most do at the present time?*

*Answer*—From the earliest traditions of the race have descended strange accounts of men who have defied the laws of age and have extended their physical existence over vast periods of time. In this day, when most people find so much to live for and learn the art of living so late in life, the matter of physical immortality assumes the proportions of a vital issue. Even science, conservative for the most part in its announcements, hints that the time may not be far off when the evils of age and decrepitude may be done away with and all men live together in a world of perpetual youth. This state should be regarded as a dream rather than a hope; but dreams, though slower of fulfillment than hopes, may in time come true.

The matter of rejuvenation, as it now stands, is no magic formula of physical immortality, but rather an effort to increase the normal span of human usefulness to a term more reasonable to the state of man. The human being, the most intelligent of the animals, is surrounded by inferior creatures whose span of life is much greater than his own. It does seem a little strange that man can have but three score years of usefulness, and the whale can sport for centuries in his ocean home. The only conclusions that seem reasonable indicate that man, through his unintelligent theory of living, shortens his own span and heaps upon himself most of the infirmities that corrupt his later years.

There is no reason why man should not enjoy good health, even under present conditions, for at least one full century, and five hundred years would not be too long a life for man to visualize as a normal period. Of course man, being the only animal with the capacity for worrying, tears down much of his life by his critical and destructive thinking. Civilization, so-called, does the rest, being the most completely destructive mechanism ever devised by juvenile intelligence.

It would be wrong to say that physical immortality is probable or even possible for average persons in the modern world. We believe that something resembling physical immortality has been accomplished by the great adepts and initiates who have mastered the secrets of life; but their accomplishment in no way justifies ordinary men and women in expecting eternal youth. Several metaphysical cults and isms have preached physical immortality, and have even tried to conceal the death of their leaders, but none of these groups has yet been able, even temporarily, to cheat the grave. The average citizen of the modern world may look forward to an increasing knowledge concerning the laws of life, and a consistent program for the lengthening of human life by scientific means. Only a very highly advanced metaphysician can reasonably expect more than the scientific form of rejuvenation, but there is every reason to believe that by the end of the present century, methods will be perfected to add from ten to twenty years of useful and efficient living to the average person's mortal span.

As to the desirability of eternal life, one has only to read the story of the *Wandering Jew,* by Eugene Sue, to get an excellent psychological picture of the curse of eternal physical existence. The body is the prison of the spirit, and it is a foolish man who would choose to spend eternity in prison. Eternal physical existence is not a possibility. The universe could allow no such tragedy to occur. Even the worlds are forever coming and going, and there is nothing eternal but spirit and space. Every reasonable method of extending physical life to the fullest of its potential span may be regarded as progressive and constructive, but to dream of an endless living in this vale shows little vision of the greater purposes of life and evolution.

A man of letters not long ago hazarded the opinion that, considering the length of time devoted to the periods of development and growth, the human being should live about four hundred years. Strangely enough, there is no historical example of a human being achieving this length of life in the last several thousand years. Of course, in the metaphysical traditions, we find records of what Thomas Vaughan, the Rosicrucian initiate, called "long livers," but the occult tradition is not accepted by modern science. There are records, however, of men whose lives have exceeded 200 years, and a goodly number who have reached 150. China has produced an unusual number of very aged persons, and it might be well to consider some of the factors involved in the achievement of an unusual span of life.

Two factors immediately present themselves. In the first place, some achieve great age by virtue of constitution. The

body seems to be born with an unusual capacity for endurance. The second factor is cultivation and discipline. By
a certain program of carefully studied action, the natural span
is increased and efficiency continued far beyond the generally
accepted boundaries. The Chinese formula for longevity is
extremely simple and has unusual merit in the light of our
present uncertain generation. The Taoists of China, among
whom are to be found a host of centenarians, gave as the first
key to extensive living the formula: do not worry. To use
an old adage, most people use up the second half of life in
the first half. Excess of emotion, inordinate ambitions, the
psychological acceptance of responsibilities, attachments, and
all the vast army of concerns that bow us down, carve huge
slices from our later years. Every time we become fussed
and bothered, we shorten life and destroy the tranquility of
the years we do not destroy.

In the Taoist belief, nothing is important. In their opinion,
the most serious thing that can happen to anyone is to die,
and even that is not important. There is nothing worth fret-
ting over or hastening after. Things you do not have are
responsibilities escaped. High rank you cannot achieve is disaster avoided. Man's wants are many, but his needs are few,
and the Taoist makes the goal of his life to live without effort,
without stress, and without strain. He moves slowly and
methodically, without tension and without nerves, to whatever end he desires to accomplish, always careful that his
ends are few. If a Taoist by some miracle finds himself in a
position of responsibility, his first task is to remove the consciousness of responsibility in himself. Wherever he is, he is
unconcerned. He does everything as wisely as he can, and then
immediately dismisses the entire matter from his mind. Rich
or poor, befriended or alone, old or young, he lives in the
same sense of detachment. He wastes no energy and permits

nothing to irritate him. In this way, he overcomes most of the causes of rapid decay.

Very few people wear out; most of them rot out. The life is corroded by acids of disposition. Strength is wasted toward ends that are not real or valuable. Most men die from the exhaustion attendant upon the effort to live. But the Chinese sage lives without effort. He seldom practices great physical exercise; in fact, he avoids every type of exertion. He never wonders about what he does, nor fears the results of his thoughts or deeds. He lives by a formula of right. He never departs from it, and he never concerns himself with evils that may come to him. With this formula, he may find himself hale and hearty at 150, frequently sought for advice, regarded as a paragon of the virtues, and entirely comfortable.

Another way of stating the Taoist formula is that every individual should be like water, for this fluid fits itself into any container without discomfort, flows into low and simple places without despair, and in the end mingles with the universal waters without regret. Placidity is power, relaxation is length of years, detachment is health. To sum up, it is only a Taoist, or one of similar accomplishment, who takes the sting out of life and is fitted to endure the years.

# SOCIAL AND POLITICAL
# PROBLEMS

## PART EIGHT

*QUESTION—What form of government—monarchy, aristocracy, democracy, or communism—is the best?*

*Answer*—It is not the form of government, but the integrity of the governing power, that is of the greatest significance. Any form of government will succeed if it is administered justly and unselfishly. No form of government will succeed when the governing power exploits its citizenry or sacrifices the common good to its own selfish purposes or policies. According to Plato, there are three forms of government in the world, only three forms possible to man. Each of these, justly administered, will bring prosperity and peace to both the governing power and the body governed. Each also, if abused, will bring misery and ultimate destruction.

The first form, according to Plato, is monarchy, the rulership by one. This, by perversion, becomes tyranny. The second form of government is aristocracy, rulership by a certain part of the people. This, by perversion, becomes oligarchy or class oppression. The third form of government is the commonwealth, or the government by all the people, and this, by perversion, becomes a chaos in which the unfit, by their majority in number, reduce the state to impotency and ultimate oblivion.

219

What we commonly call socialism, or communism, is an aspect of the commonwealth described by Plato. It is rulership by all, but for its success it demands the intelligence and integrity of all. A commonwealth, or democracy, or socialist government can succeed only when each citizen elevates the common good above his own advantage, thinking first of his neighbor and his country, and of himself only after the common issues have been solved.

Philosophy teaches that, because of the imperfect state of man, and because of the evident and inevitable inequality throughout nature, it is not possible for all men to rule, nor is it desirable that the state shall rest its security in the keeping of the great mass of comparatively immature and unlearned people. Philosophy therefore teaches that, at this stage of human evolution, the best form of government is that in which the wisest people of any state or country rule or lead; those less informed should cooperate by giving their allegiance and obeying the laws that have been established by those of greater wisdom and vision. Plato called this system *government by the philosophic elect.* It will yet be demonstrated in society that this is the only system whereby all men may participate together in the wisdom and safety of enlightened leadership. There are only a few great, wise, and good men in the world at any one time. Under our present systems of government, these men are seldom called to high stations of leadership, the governments of the world being dominated by cliques of professional politicians. When the wisest lead, then the most rapid progress is assured. When the uninformed lead, civilization loses purpose and perspective. And when those of ulterior motive lead, men live in fear and uncertainty, victimized by the ambitions of unscrupulous tyrants and despots.

A people capable of self-government requires little govern-ment and few laws. Many laws demoralize the state and bring with them the psychology of servility and oppression. Let the laws be few and good, let the people respect their leaders, and the leaders earn the respect of their people. Nations will then flourish, peace will abound, and the pros-perity of empires will be assured.

*QUESTION—What is the proper philosophical attitude to-ward war?*

*Answer*—All great systems of religion and philosophy agree that war is the greatest collective misfortune with which humanity is afflicted. Yet wars have constantly plagued hu-mankind since the days of the Atlantean conquerors, and have come to be regarded as essential elements of progress. Most of the nations of the modern world have had their origins in war, have sustained their separate policies by the power of arms, and are threatened with annihilation if they relax their armaments. The general lack of understanding between races and nations, and selfish, aggressive attitudes of so many of the world powers, have resulted in a general world acceptance of the inevitability of war.

With the virtues of heroism sung to the youth of every nation, and war condoned as a necessary evil, the way of the peace-lover is hard. Under the name of patriotism, young men are invited to perpetuate racial antagonisms and national feuds. The civilizing influences of education and culture have subdued and transmuted much of the barbarism of primi-tive humanity, but war has resisted all mellowing and refining influences and, with each passing generation, scientific de-

structiveness assumes more frightful and devastating proportions. In this day, peace is on the lips of all, but hate is in
the hearts of so many that it appears that much more suffering must come to the world before mankind can turn from
hating to the arts of peace.

It is difficult to set a fixed standard to be followed by each
man in his attitude toward war. After all, standards of right
and wrong are individual problems, based on the highest
conviction of the individual. Certain classes of mankind believe in war, prefer combat to peaceful living, and measure
superiority in terms of combativeness. Only ages of experience and suffering can mature such types to the degree that
they will understand and appreciate gentler standards of living. Then there is another type of humanity that accepts war
as a personal responsibility and, from patriotic motives, is
willing to go forth and die for the generals, or the dictators,
or the munition manufacturers. This level of mankind may
be naturally peace-loving, home-loving, and noncombative
in its personal relationships, but under the spell of patriotic
fervor may elevate war to the plane of a divine necessity and
march forth to death, martyr to gods of conflict. There
is a third class of people who, thoroughly disgusted and disillusioned as to both the causes and effects of war, feel that
it is virtuous and right to protect home and country from the
aggressions of other militant powers. This is the entirely
defensive attitude and, by most progressive thinkers, is accepted as the highest standard possible under existing world
conditions. Then there is the last group, composed of avowed
pacifists who refuse to participate in any form of military
conflict, regardless of motives, causes or circumstances. This
last group is steadily increasing in society and will in time
exert a powerful influence in the affairs of nations.

The peace-loving citizen of any so-called civilized nation is concerned with one almost insurmountable obstacle to his pacifist desires. That is the system of compulsory militarism which forces him into war whether he will or not. Of course, if he refuses to fight, in the face of this law, he may be imprisoned or, in extreme cases, even executed. It is very hard to be sane in a crazy world, and minorities, even though they be right, are nearly always the victims of majorities, especially in so-called democratic nations.

The metaphysical philosopher, faced with the problem of war, has one of two courses open to him. The first is to openly avow his pacifism and bear cheerfully and resignedly the abuses that will be heaped upon him; or he may volunteer for some line of service in which his duties are of a constructive rather than a destructive nature. If he cannot prevent war, he may be able to contribute some peace or security to those afflicted by war. The medical corps, hospitalization work, and other lines concerned with the reclamation of destroyed and demoralized health or courage, offer constructive work and a field of very great and real service.

The philosopher does not approve of war, but he cannot always prevent war. He must realize that his greatest field of work is educational. In times of peace, he can teach the follies of war. In times of war, he can teach the blessings of peace. His own actions in the emergency of war will be considerably influenced by the circumstances and conditions of the hour. But under all conditions, he must strive to the fullest possible degree to promote the well-being and enlightenment of all with whom he comes in contact.

*QUESTION—Should an idealist enter politics?*

*Answer*—It is a sad day for government when such a question concerns public mind. Theoretically speaking, the idealist belongs in politics. There is no science that needs progressive idealism more desperately than the science of statesmanship. Yet, to succeed in the science of government, an idealist must possess practical experience. Otherwise he may ruin not only his own life but the life of the whole empire as well. Unfortunately, when we think of an idealist, we generally think of an individual hopelessly lacking practical and provident virtues. He possesses the qualities of the poet and the inventor, and suffers the general condemnation that is heaped upon both these abstractionists because of their lack of realism.

In modern politics, what is generally meant by an idealist is an honest man, a truthful, upright person shipwrecked in a sea of intrigues and perversity. Honesty used to be regarded as a homely, human virtue, but now, in politics, it is defined as an abstract, impractical menace to the present methods of accomplishing results. In recent years, honesty has been devaluated to the vanishing point, and in political leadership is regarded as a potential detriment to advancement and success.

Idealists are, for the most part, noncombative persons, ill framed by nature for stratagems and spoils. For this reason, they find it exceedingly difficult to cope with dishonesty, for, not having enough of it in themselves, they do not know how to recognize it in others. Therefore, honesty becomes their undoing, and in the end they are nicely "framed" by their political associates and made to appear the most dishonest reprobates of all. It has well been said, if you have a good reputation and wish to keep it, stay out of politics.

It is easy to see, therefore, why politicians draw to themselves others of like and equally shady character. It is also easy to see why politics go from bad to worse, until communities are bowed to despair under the corruption of their governors. Yet, this very disease of corrupted leadership shows how desperately a remedy is needed.

If a man has courage of conviction, an unshakeable integrity, and has dreams for a better state of man, with sufficient practical experience to build adequate foundations under his dreams, his place is in politics. But he must be prepared to fight for his life and reputation. He must be prepared to sacrifice his wealth, his peace of mind, and possibly his good name in the desperate struggle against overwhelming odds. He must attempt all this with the realization that he has only a fighting chance of success, and no probabilities of either recognition or reward. He must also fully realize that the constituency for which he is sacrificing so much will neither appreciate nor support him, and that in time of trouble he can only turn inward for strength and encouragement. He must realize that he has not made an easy or glamorous choice, but is opposing with his single strength the selfish stupidity and corruption of one of the most powerful organizations in the world—the body politic.

Political science had its origin in the complex of social problems arising in national and racial civilization. Laws are rules of contact and relationship, founded upon necessity and intended to sustain individual and collective integrity. As the majority of human beings are neither wholly wise, nor wholly honest, grievous evils have arisen. Ambitious men have perverted the interpretations of law to their own profit and, having achieved positions of power and authority, have made other laws for their own advantage at the expense of the public good. There is scarcely a time to be found in history when the political systems of so-called civilized nations were not corrupt. Yet in the face of this general perversion, it still remains evident that laws are necessary, that government is necessary. The individual must be protected against the schemes of his neighbors and the corruptions within himself.

Although most politicians are insincere, political science itself is useful and necessary at this stage in human development. It is natural, therefore, that wise men should desire to correct the evident defects in political systems, so that mankind may enjoy the protection of honest and efficient codes and statutes. I cannot see how it is possible for a philosopher to ignore the evident need for political reform. At the same time, it is painfully apparent that the wise, being utterly in the minority, can accomplish little by attacking and decrying existing evils.

Nearly all the great world teachers realized that the majority of mankind was not sufficiently evolved to solve its vital problems with philosophy alone. The majority benefits most through the correction of the social and economic ills that oppress the people. Buddha bitterly attacked the political theocracy of India, striking at the very soul of political privilege when he attcked the caste system. Socrates paid with his life for his bitter denunciation of the Athenian policy of privileges and the delinquency of legislators. Confucius devoted his life to the reformation of the philosophies and political institutions of China. Zarathustra first converted the king to his doctrine so that he might begin his reformations with state. Moses and Aaron defied the Pharaoh of Egypt, and Judaism arose on a foundation of social reforms fully equal in significance to the religious purposes. Six of the

Seven Sophists of Greece were legislators and political reformists, as were also Pythagoras and Plato. It is generally acknowledged that Jesus was a reformer of Jewish social and political law, and Mohammed fearlessly attacked the whole legislative theory of Arabia, denouncing the privileges of the Meccans, and established a doctrine that not only dominates Arabia but encroaches upon every social and political aspect of Islamic life.

It is the duty of the philosopher to labor unselfishly and devotedly for the promulgation of truth, wisdom and justice. He must perforce withdraw his support from any individual or institution that functions inconsistently with reasonable standards of integrity. On the other hand, political corruptions, like ignorance, (of which they are a part), cannot actually be remedied by legislation, but must be finally corrected by the improvement of human nature itself. Therefore, the philosopher may say, "I cannot make a man honest, but if I can dispel ignorance he will become honest himself." Philosophy always approaches the political problem from an educational viewpoint. If we can make enough people see the reality of those great laws of life which circumscribe all mundane affairs, they will live better as individuals. The integrity of the individual is the cornerstone of social and political well-being.

*QUESTION—How can we live a spiritual life in a materialistic world?*

*Answer*—The secret of spiritual security is detachment. In a sense, every age is materialistic, yet in each of the civilizations of humanity, and in each of the periods of history, great saints, sages, and saviors have risen out of the racial level and taken their places among the immortals. It is not the world we live in that counts; it is the way we live in the world that is important. The world presses in upon us to the degree that we respond to the emotion of attachment. As long as accumulation dominates the purpose for living, men will remain oppressed by their environments and limited by their times. Yet in philosophical matters, possession does not inspire superiority. Great thinkers seldom arise from the moneyed classes. The rich are too burdened by their possessions. They have neither time nor energy left with which to contemplate the philosophic truths of life. While the poor long for wealth and the rich long for peace, and those of moderate condition long for everything—the spiritual equation is accorded little consideration.

Most religious people attempt to combine a search for spiritual improvement with a frenzied effort to build up the economic standing. Such a division of energies results in a general chaos. When the question is asked, "How can I live a spiritual life in a materialistic age?" the questioner frequently means: "How can I be enlightened and enriched at the same time?"

Some convenient little "metaphysical" organizations have sprung up to assure a certain type of humanity that the universe is particularly interested in the financial standing of aspiring souls, and that "illumination" insures an ever-flowing fountain of wealth, happiness and personal magnetism. The profound thinker, however, is not deceived by such pretenses. The sage knows that he cannot serve God and Mammon at the same time. Therefore, he withdraws from the psychology of economics, and sets about the task of perfecting his own life through the mastery of appetites and desires.

Moderation is the beginning of wisdom. Those satisfied with nothing are the salt of the earth. Philosophy does not teach improvidence or the neglect of responsibilities, but it would temper those inordinate ambitions which inevitably lead to ruin. Developing more and more of inward consciousness, the aspirant to spiritual things lives less and less in the material world, demands little from it, and is not deceived by its appearances. A man can live spiritually in this generation if he will make spirituality the purpose of his living and will sacrifice to that purpose the less worthy aims. Materiality is necessary to spiritual accomplishment. The physical world is the ante-chamber to the Temple of the Mysteries. Those who cannot pass the tests of living, cannot expect to enter the House of the Mysteries.

*QUESTION—Would you advise a man to leave civilization who cannot make spiritual progress among a corrupt and evil populace?*

*Answer*—It is not possible for anyone to run away from life. There is an old Arabian fable of a man who sought to escape from the evils of existence, only to discover that the shadow of them pursued him to the most distant parts of the earth. At last he learned that this shadow was his own body, and that the one evil no man can escape is himself. Philosophy does not advise truth seekers to run away from experience, but rather to use wisdom to face experience more intelligently. These stirring and difficult times in which we live are important to the soul growth of each individual. Philosophy is not merely a studying of books or a thinking of beautiful thoughts. Philosophy is living well in a world that tests the capacity of the individual to live well. Life itself is an initiation into the sanctuary of the Divine Mystery. As neophytes of old were tested as to courage, integrity, and wisdom by various trials devised by the priests, so modern truth seekers are tested by the adversity of life. An individual who cannot achieve where he is cannot achieve anywhere else. Achievement is an inner strength rising up secure and sufficient. Strength comes from action and adversity. The years ahead will be trying years. The steel of the human soul is tempered by the flame of suffering.

*QUESTION—To what degree is a university education useful to a person interested in the perfecting of his inner spiritual life?*

*Answer*—The answer to this question must be understood to be an entirely individual matter. To some, higher educational opportunity is of the greatest importance, whereas to others it is comparatively meaningless. Education does not insure spiritual superiority; that is, the type of education to be secured from our colleges. On the other hand, education can bestow capacity and appreciation, and, all things being equal, may be an aid to the appreciation of metaphysical values. The ancients regarded education as a prerequisite to philosophy. Pythagoras would accept no disciples who had not achieved scholastic honors; and Plato caused a panel to be placed over the gate of his school on which were the words: "Let no man ignorant of geometry enter here." The value of so-called higher education depends upon the motive that moves the student to learning, and also the mental capacity of the student himself. Of course, youth is without the experience necessary for the higher appreciation of educational opportunity, and very few college students are moved to their studies by any great spiritual aspiration. It is only years afterwards, when most of the schooling has been forgotten, that the mature person begins to wish that he had been more attentive in his periods of learning.

One of our greatest students of comparative religion and philosophy was deprived by poverty of the benefits of a university education. General Albert Pike, soldier, scholar, philosopher and Freemason, was turned from the house of learning because he could not pay the matriculation fee. Thus denied, he educated himself and became one of the greatest scholars of the modern world. In his advancing years, the university which had refused him admission offered him an honorary degree. Pike declined, saying that when he needed the university it had refused him, and that he now had no use for its honors. After his sixtieth year, he mastered the Hebrew language, also the Persian tongue, and Sanskrit, and translated the sacred scriptures of the Jews, Persians, and Hindus, with numerous important commentaries.

Education is necessary to philosophy, but education is not always to be secured from those institutions presumably dedicated to its promulgation. The shallowness of our present educational theory means, usually, dubious returns for the years spent in the modern college.

*QUESTION—How can we solve religious differences in the home?*

*Answer*—Religious differences in the home are much more apt to be theoretical than truly spiritual. Religion may be defined as veneration for God, the love of beauty, and the doing of good works. Such a code cannot conflict with any enlightened system of religion, and therefore so-called religious differences are illusionary rather than real. Bigoted people, clinging to the jot and tittle of some narrow creed, are naturally and inevitably intolerant because of the smallness of their viewpoint. Such individuals are very difficult to get along with if you attempt to argue them out of their notions or impose a new religious concept upon their thinking. But even these people usually mean well. They often sacrifice and suffer in a sincere effort to live up to (or down to) the dogmas they have accepted. Sincerity is a virtue that must not be despised, even if certain forms of it are distinctly annoying.

The metaphysician, however, has his own peculiar faults, and is seldom faultless in his interpretation of religious ethics. So-called "progressive thinkers" are frequently an intolerant group, despising the opinions of conservatives, and making themselves generally obnoxious among people whose opinions differ from their own. If the metaphysician resents efforts to impose the orthodox upon his mind, he must remember that orthodox people are equally disinclined to accept beliefs which they regard as heretical and dangerous.

Philosophy teaches that a man's religious life is strictly a personal matter. No one has a right to dictate to another what his religious beliefs should be. But true metaphysics is an interpretation rather than a cult and, if properly used, does not conflict with or discredit any system of religious thought. The purpose of philosophy is to bring not arguments but fuller understanding, deeper appreciation, and a fuller and more perfect tolerance.

If you are studying metaphysics and your belief is opposed by the members of your family, or causes dissension and unpleasantness in your daily life through the interference of others, remember this—metaphysics is an inner experience. No one needs to know that you are a metaphysician. Let others observe only that you live more nobly and more honestly; that you are more gentle and kindly; that a new wisdom has come to you; that you no longer worry, fret and argue; that you live a happy, normal and contented life. If your metaphysical interests are evidenced by these improvements in yourself, there is little likelihood that your beliefs will be very heartily opposed. It is when we talk incessantly of noble things, and live unpleasant and obnoxious lives, that people become irritated with our words because our deeds are so different.

To harp continuously on mystical platitudes, and fail in the daily problems of life, discredits the individual and casts a reflection upon the doctrine he claims to believe. Live ignobly, and no one is interested in your religion; live nobly and beautifully, and all men will desire the secret of your living. Let your life, and not your lips, bear witness to your doctrines. Then you can mingle with all faiths and beliefs of men, and live side by side with those of different opinions. All men admire improvement, but they are tired of platitudes that bring no change in conduct. Do not try to convert people—just convert yourself—and things are liable to turn out well in the end.


*QUESTION—Should religion be taught in the public schools?*


*Answer*—Religion should most certainly be taught in the public schools—but *religion*, not *theology*. Religion, in the proper sense of the word, is spiritual ethics, and its foundation is the teaching of the broad principles of right and wrong, absolutely indispensable to constructive and successful living. Theology, on the other hand, divided as it is into innumerable sects and isms, cannot be taught in the public schools of any democratic or liberal-thinking country.

In ancient times, religious education was part of the national life in highly civilized countries. The religion of the country was the State Religion. Where State Religion existed, morality and ethics were the very foundation of education, and standards of integrity were comparatively higher among educated people than they are under our present system of divorcing religious influence from the state.

Our highly diversified background complicates the religious problem in the United States. Parents representing over two hundred and fifty sects and creeds, send their children to public schools, and must be assured that nothing will be taught to these children that will conflict with the creedal religious training that they receive, or should receive, in their homes. Baptist parents do not want their children to be taught Methodist doctrines. The Presbyterians will have no Mormonism inculcated upon their children, and the orthodox Jewish families will court no Roman Catholicism influencing the formative minds of their offspring. This has been a stalemate in religious education, with the result that the young hopefuls graduate from the public school entirely devoid of ethics and are ready to swell the ranks of first offenders in those thousands of petty misdemeanors that are the first steps to careers of crime and perversion.

The trouble has been, first, that the religious education which the school is not permitted to give, is also (in the majority of cases) neglected in the home or presented in such narrow, sectarian terms that the children themselves revolt against the bigotry of the older generation, and so have no religious ethics to direct their codes of living. Also, it is a mistake to believe that religious education needs to interfere with the theological limitations of any personal perspective. No matter how narrow and intolerant a person is in religious matters, he will generally uphold the Ten Commandments and the Golden Rule. There is sufficient religious material common to all the sects of Christendom, Judaism, and other religious groups, to permit of sound religious education that conflicts with nothing and can accomplish only good.

All religions worthy of the name of religion acknowledge the existence of a Supreme Principle of good, which controls the universe with law and order and decrees that men shall live together honestly, justly, and benevolently. All religions commonly concur in the teaching that a virtuous life is acceptable and necessary; and that justice and honesty in relationships and dealings promote the spiritual state and preserve human society. A beautiful religious outline could be formed acceptable to all, and be the common denominator of the religious life of the country. Children could be given this liberal education, and the result would be a marked decrease in juvenile delinquency and human unhappiness.

Of course, the teaching of comparative religion in the higher grades of the educational system would be a most important step forward in the civilizing of humanity. But this cannot come yet. Much intolerance and bigotry must first be done away with. The partial remedy here suggested must be the first step. The spiritual ideals of the race must find some common denominator from which to work. A simple but vital truth, such as the Golden Rule, could be that common denominator. In time, comparative religion will probably have precedence over many of the so-called practical sciences in the field of education. No individual who does not understand the several great religions of the world has any right to regard himself as educated, for in spite of all the industrial and mechanical emphasis of the last few generations, religion and religious thought are still the greatest moving forces in humanity—the greatest living power of the world. To study the Greeks and not their religions, is foolish. To study India, China, Egypt and Rome, without mastering their history, their ethics and esthetics, is to leave out of education the very soul and essence of it. Involved problems of comparative religion belong, of course, in the higher grades of education; but the beginnings of inter-religious understanding should be included with the ABC's and the three R's.

*QUESTION—Is marriage a physical or spiritual union? And what about divorce?*

*Answer*—In common with all the other Sacraments of ancient religious institutions, the ceremony of marriage is a symbolic ritual. It rests with the two who are joined together, whether or not spiritual values play a part in marital relationship. Whether the bond of marriage is solemnized by the clergy, or merely legalized by a Justice of the Peace, can have little bearing upon the integrity or permanence of vows or obligations. The spiritual life of man is not in the keeping of either the church or the state. Each human being is his own high priest, and only the obligations he makes to himself are real. Marriage is blessed only by the sincerity and devotion of those two who mingle their lives in a common destiny. Marriage is no more permanent, and no more sacred, than the standards and ideals of the man and wife.

Lawgivers of the ancient world established the laws of marriage to promote monogamy, and established responsibility for the protection and education of children. The home was designed as a perfect institution, the unit of measurement for nation and empire. But a home is not a home simply because of the laws of the nation, or the religious opinions of the day. If the home fails within itself, it is the worst form of stupidity to force uncongenial people to remain under the same roof for the sake of the dignity of conventions.

Under our present social psychology, mismating is the general order of things. Successful marriages are the exception. The factors that contribute to the permanance of the home are disappearing from our daily life. Under such conditions it is frequently impossible to preserve a home, or to reorganize one that has been broken by divergent opinions. Two people starting from a certain point may develop unequally, so that their interests diverge through the years until in the end nothing remains in common. This cannot be prevented, and life together under such conditions is frequently unbearable. For two people to live together, under such conditions, is more dangerous to the spiritual life than an amicable and intelligent termination of the whole affair.

In the matter of divorce, children are usually the greatest sufferers, but under some conditions, divorce is even better for the child. A child may be better off without any father, than with a drunken or abusive one, and separate maintenance is often the lesser of two evils. This does not mean that homes should be broken over trivial and inconsequential differences, or that a home is necessarily impossible for individuals of different mind and opinion. If, however, the sympathies die out, if respect and affection have been hopelessly broken, a separation is the only reasonable and sensible procedure.

It has been observed that the successful home is to a con-siderable degree the result of education. The percentage of divorces among graduates of universities that teach eugenics, is much smaller than among graduates of schools omitting this important subject. Young people woefully uninformed on the responsibilities of marriage contribute heavily to the income of divorce attorneys. Divorce, like every other insti-tution devised to remedy evils in society, is frequently abused. It is far less disgraceful, however, to come forward openly and acknowledge that it is necessary to remedy a mistake, than it is to suffer through the years in the silent pathetic way of the orthodox-ridden centuries that have preceded us.

The ceremony of marriage, if simply and sincerely per-formed, may serve as an inspiration and guide through the years to come. It is wise to remind young people of the dignity and solemnity of the step they are taking. The good thoughts of well-wishers may be a source of power, and beauty of the occasion satisfies the esthetic impulse, giving the union the advantage of culture and refinement. But as surely as a funeral service cannot insure the future of the dead, so surely a marriage ceremony cannot insure the harmony of the living. It is not a God in the heavens, but the God in the heart, which sanctifies the institutions of men.

From an occult standpoint, the association of lives is a necessary step in the evolution of humanity. Each person, being in himself androgynous, possesses a male-female na-ture; one objective and the other subjective, according to the sex. Thus in the male, the female nature is latent but not absent, and in the female, the male nature is latent but like-wise subjectively present. Through association, the objective nature of each is complemented by the objective nature of the other—the result being an androgynous unit composed of half of the male and half of the female. Everyone has observed how persons long married take on each other's mannerisms and to some degree even appearances. Through marriage each of the parties is gradually building up the latent part of himself, as decreed by the law of nature. Man unfolds esthetic powers, developing his intuition and imagination. Woman is unfolding intellectual powers, strengthening her reason and individuality.

The doctrine of soul-mates is not accepted in the great schools of philosophy. The sexes are equal and complete in their spiritual parts. Each soul is perfecting itself from association with the other, but it should not be believed that the two will ever merge into one. Rather, each is becoming in itself a perfect whole, and by so doing, is united in the end with the Universal One, which is the Cause and Ultimate of existence.

*QUESTION—To what extent are parents responsible for the lives of their children?*

*Answer*—Of all the animal kingdom man is the most helpless in his infancy. For many long years, his survival depends upon the assistance of those about him. A child's well-being is the special responsibility of his parents. It is their duty to preserve its life through infancy, and shield it from the adversities of life until it becomes capable of controlling its own destiny. Parents must view this responsibility as a debt they owe to nature. Each human being pays the debt for his own birth and up-bringing by sacrificing in his own turn for those whom he brings into the world.

The process of birth, with its attendant growth and development, is the only way in which human beings can come into this world, but it is a mistake for parents to assume possessive attitudes toward their children, nor are children indebted to parents beyond a reasonable degree of appreciation. Parents do not own their children; rather, it is their duty to assist and direct the unfolding life until this life is capable of directing its own destiny. A certain veneration is natural to man, and it is proper that a child should appreciate the struggles and the suffering the parents pass through to give it opportunities in life. Parental responsibility ends when the child reaches majority. It is then a free agent to live as it pleases, and interference with its life beyond that point usually does more harm than good. If a child has been brought up wisely and honestly until majority, its character is usually set in paths of integrity. Children who disappoint their parents later in life, have usually been disappointed in their parents earlier in life. Very often our own mistakes live in our children.

A father or mother who constantly reminds a grown son or daughter of an eternal indebtedness to parents, is guilty of a serious mistake, which frequently ends in tragedy. Parents who earn the respect of their children are usually respected and honored, but nagging, overshadowing parents must look forward to lonely years. It is the duty of the parent to sow the seeds of integrity in the child's life, to train the child wisely and gently, and then to release it and send it forth into the world to live its own life.

According to philosophy, incarnating souls are drawn into families in order to receive types of experience that they have earned in previous lives. Very often, spiritually, the child is older than the parent, and it is, of course, entirely erroneous to view the new-born infant as newly formed by the hand of God. Children are usually attracted to parents whose

level of consciousness is similar to their own, or who offer
the opportunities for the payment of a certain specific type of
karma. This is the reason for the saying: "like father like
son." This is also the reason why parents so frequently find
their own worst faults perpetuated in their progeny. This is
not due to heredity, but to the principle that "like attracts
like," and souls needing certain types of experience are drawn
to homes where this experience is to be found.

Parents who abuse, neglect, or mistreat their children may
look forward to the same kind of treatment themselves in
future lives. Parents who cling to their children, warping
their destinies and denying them freedom of experience, will
suffer from the same factors when they come into the world
again. A skeptic on the subject of reincarnation once asked
why so many tragedies occur to small children, themselves
incapable of reasoning out the responsibility for their own
actions. The suffering which children pass through is usually
the results of actions performed in a previous life. A parent
who neglects his child may be born a neglected child. Parents
who nag their children may be born into a home where there
are nagging parents, for whatever we do, that in turn shall
be done unto us. Therefore the parent who seriously and conscientiously fulfills his duties and responsibilities, not only does
that which is right according to the law of life, but makes
easy his own way in lives to come.

QUESTION—*The code of morals that guided the older
generation is breaking down. What will be the new standard
of personal conduct?*

*Answer*—For nearly two thousand years, Western civilization has been dominated by the moral force of Christian

theology. The essential doctrines of Christianity were founded in the Mosaic law, the principal modification being the recognition of the esthetic or cultural factor. Christian theology was devised by a special class in society and imposed upon the rest, so that it did not represent an honest social trend. In its beginning, the Christian code was extremely simple, and particularly evident was its lack of originality and inspiration. It was developed with an almost ferocious literalism. Everything subtle or controversial or individual was eliminated, and the code of conduct assumed the proportions of an infallible revelation. The element of growth has always been lacking in the Christian theology, and this shortening of perspective produced first inhibition, and then rebellion.

Modern society is emerging from the Dark Ages of theological inhibition. The standards of morality are shifting from formula to fact. The old church first arbitrarily defined the universe and its laws, and then set itself to the task of bending all human spirits to this preconceived pattern. Modern society realizes that a considerable part of the so-called Christian code of conduct is the product of a type of mind incapable of seeing life honestly, and incapable of courageously facing the larger inferences of personal action and personal freedom. We have only to study the lives of the early theologians to realize that they would be incapable of formulating a broad, deep, and understanding philosophy of conduct. Theology is actually based upon a theory of introversion, limitation, and repression. The "thou-shalt-not" idea puts everything into the negative, so that from the first the mind is turned from normalcy to stilted, circumscribed, and narrowed interpretations.

Philosophy differs from religion particularly in its acceptance of the integrity of life. Theology, overwhelmed with the magnitude of evil, devotes too much of its time to the problem of original and secondary sin to perceive the sincere and profound values of life. Philosophy, having no doctrine of original sin, and acknowledging no principle of evil in the world, sees the mistakes of man as sharing a common divinity with his good deeds. Mistakes are inevitable in the process of growing; but the philosopher sees something divine even in the errors of the race, while the theologian sees something infernal even in its virtues.

The focus of culture is moving gradually toward the East. Psychology is intrinsic to Eastern culture, whereas in the West it is assumed to be something outside and apart, to be mastered only with the greatest effort. The Western mind has not learned to think naturally in terms of fact. It has been long confused by artificial and superficial standards. The shift from a Western to an Eastern basis means a change from a collective to an individual or personal code of ethics. The Eastern philosopher thinks of life as flowing from himself, whereas the Westerner thinks of life as an ocean in which he is immersed. The Eastern classics find space, creation, and all the laws of being within the Self, and the Western thinker sees himself as an infinitesimal speck in the midst of an immeasurable existence. The Easterner, therefore, has more courage than the Westerner. In fact, to the Westerner, the Oriental has a sublime audacity which gives him the right to live above the law, or with himself as the law, instead of merely one who bends eternally to the whims of God or state.

The Chinese philosophy of conduct is possibly a rounded statement of what the West is groping for. China moved from a theological to a philosophical foundation in prehistoric times, experiencing in almost forgotten ages what we are struggling through today. Taoism is the mature product of mature thinking. It is without illusion, but it did not fall into a crassness as the Western extremist has a tendency to do. The beginning of the Taoist's code of life is his realization of what life is and the ability to accept it on a moderate level of significance. The Taoist refuses to be overwhelmed by life; he refuses to be drowned in a sea of circumstance or to drown himself in the torrent of his own outpourings. To him creation, life, and experience are so terribly real and so profoundly deep, that there is nothing he can do about them except realize them, without any effort to mold them, change them, modify them, or resist them.

The Taoist's viewpoint would be very unsafe if he did not have a profound realization of his fundamental premise, for inaction can arise either from the grossest ignorance or the deepest wisdom. When the Westerner faces life, he immediately wonders what he can do about it, but the Easterner, realizing that no one can do anything about it, develops the qualities of an exquisite acceptance and accomplishes a very strange but, when understood, deeply significant tranquillity toward both inward and outward matters.

The untrained person cannot easily appreciate the integrity of the Chinese sage, but flourishing under his own philosophy, the Celestial enjoys a hundred and fifty to two hundred and fifty years of life without the friction of resisting inevitables or the corruption of complaint, strivings, yearnings or petulance. It is not a life of inertia, but a life of action based upon an adequate viewpoint, and therefore restricted in nothing, limited in nothing, and with no temptation to excess in anything—a difficult viewpoint to attain, but astonishingly subtle when attained.

The first principle of the Taoist code is an acceptance of fact—fact in its most brutal and uncolored form. Fact becomes the foundation of philosophy, and nothing is believed or admitted to the belief that is inconsistent with fact. Fact is made the ideal. It is neither realism nor idealism, as we know it, for the *real* becomes the ideal; the ideal becomes the *real;* and the fundamental confusion that besets the West is cured at its very beginning.

Applied to Western living and thinking, philosophy advances the premise that the confusion of living is largely the result of building up inadequate foundations, or foundations colored and distorted by specialized intepretation. Nothing is as noble as truth, nothing is as adequate as truth, and nothing more difficult to discover. Yet, in the end, no elaborate structure of belief can be more permanent than the creed of truth itself. Not theologically speaking, but ethically and culturally speaking, the fact must be the beginning. The fact is that life is; that life, as truth and as law, is flowing forever through an infinitude of modes and forms. Life itself is the fact in these modes and forms. It has its own laws and cannot be measured by any of the manifestations through which it passes. The life in man is his truth. If he ceases to exercise his own mental power of limitation, the life itself moves him, and these motions are true to the degree that he does not interfere with them. He cannot, however, accomplish life without a complete impersonalization of his viewpoint. Every mood and emotion that dominates him, even temporarily, causes him to impose his own purpose upon life. Having distorted life to his own ends, he then examines his own distortion and calls it life. Upon this distortion, he builds a system of laws, of measurement and control, but he never realizes that life itself requires no control because its every motion is intrinsic and innate Reality.

It may seem that you are wandering about in extreme abstraction, but particulars are all suspended from abstraction.

According to the flow of an entirely invisible and intangible fact, all visible and tangible matters are changed and distorted or rendered normal. The code of conduct depends upon establishing the fact of yourself. You have to go behind what you feel and behind what you think, and behind what you hope for, or even aspire to, and find what you are. If, like the Chinese philosopher, you can accomplish this, you will discover that you are an inevitable fact and must inevitably accomplish certain things, must inevitably pass through certain experiences, and must inevitably be yourself forever. The realization arising from this discovery solves in itself the thousands of secondary issues that depend upon a fundamental realization.

In the last analysis, it is not that you should do what you think you should do, or that you should not do what you think you should not do, or that you should desperately overcome this or frantically develop that—but rather *realize that you are what you are,* not apparently but factually, and that all the struggles you impose upon yourself are a wrestling with shadows. You approach realization. There is no use trying to be free. There is no such thing as freedom. There is no use trying to sustain around yourself arbitrary standards and codes —these, like freedom, have no existence. It is impossible to escape fact, and it is impossible to make any unreality permanent.

From a certain inward strength arising from the open-eyed acceptance of truth, you can build outward, tolerantly, majestically, transcendently; not by rising above things, but by rising to things, realizing that fact itself is the ultimate of height as well as the finality of endeavor. The inhibitions of society become more or less non-existent, the laws of others inconsequential; in fact too worthless to break as well as to keep. Fact within being supreme, it is not necessary to conquer the universe step by step, or to rebel against inhibitions one by one. Such striving, according to the Taoist, is very exhausting. Rather, by first destroying the illusions at their source, conduct ceases to be a problem. It is no longer necessary to say: what shall I do, or what shall I not do? The truth remains that I do what I am. Nothing else is reasonable or possible.

The only crucial matter is the original finding of the Real. If, by misfortune and the lack of discrimination, appetite or emotion is accepted as the Real, there is failure at the beginning. Only the true and absolute fact, which is the Source of All, can be the working premise. Once this is achieved, there is no problem left in life, and, lacking this achievement, there is no solution to the problem of life.

Therefore the commandment: Find the Real, and with this there is no need for other commandments, for the fact itself is vaster than all law, deeper than all understanding, and incapable of separation into ideas or preachments. It takes many laws to keep a foolish man on the path of purpose, but the wise man needs no laws at all;—he is Law.

# MISCELLANEOUS

## PART NINE

*QUESTION—What is the Philosopher's Stone?*

*Answer*—The alchemists of the Middle Ages, following the ancient formulas of Hermes the Egyptian, sought to accomplish the three ends of the Hermetic Art. The three goals of alchemical research were the Elixir of Life, the Philosopher's Stone, and the transmutation of metals. The Elixir of Life was the mysterious subtle essence that healed all disease and bestowed immortality. The Philosopher's Stone was the mysterious ruby-diamond or the blood-diamond, the Wise Man's Stone, which bestowed all knowledge and power and rulership over all the forces of nature. The transmutation of metals was the secret of regeneration, the restoration of all the corrupted values of life and security. Of course, alchemy was divine chemistry, the secret of the perfection of life through the disciplines of wisdom. The Philosopher's Stone was the perfected inner life of the individual, his own diamond soul. He who perfects his own soul possesses the touchstone of the wise. The luminous soul-aura of the enlightened human being is the symbolical diamond, and he who has achieved to it lacks nothing that is necessary to wisdom and divine authority. The laboratory is life, the retort is the body of the alchemist himself, and the mysterious processes that take place within the retort represent the transmutation of the base elements of life, brought about by the living of the divine art.

*QUESTION—Can peace in the outer life be attained without attaining peace within?*

*Answer*—To the average person peace means happiness. The term actually signifies stillness, and is the dying out of the contentions, frictions and irritations that ignorance and intemperance consistently set up in the human consciousness. There is a wonderful phrase in the Arabian Nights' Entertainment: "Happiness must be earned." In these few words is set forth the philosophical formula for well-being. In the same way, peace must be earned. It is the purpose of each evolving soul to perfect within its own nature a condition of well-being sufficient to assure tranquility and security. Peace is not in the world—it is in the soul. The contentions of outer existence cease when the soul becomes one with truth. Only when the inner life is established in wisdom can the outer life be at peace with its world.

*QUESTION—Does it harm one to attend spiritualistic meetings?*

*Answer*—In answering this question, it is not my desire to discredit the sincerity of spiritualists, but rather to point out certain hazards which believing people, enthused with an idea, are apt to overlook. A spiritualistic seance is a negative vortex of physical forces. Such a vortex draws into itself decarnate entities of various kinds, as well as numerous larvae or elementals of the astral world. The average medium has no power to control the entities that impinge themselves upon the plexus of the sympathetic nervous system. In the seance, both the medium and the sitters are helpless victims of such malefic entities as may care to attack them. Therefore, there is constant danger in seances that the sitters will take away with them elemental beings that have attached themselves to various parts of the aura. These elementals may later attack the physical resistance by sapping the etheric body. When this condition has gone on for a time, and resistance has been greatly lowered, the elemental or malicious decarnate entity may obsess the living person and finally drive the ego out of its body. While such a condition is an extreme case, it is a hazard that every person must be prepared to face who encourages any form of negative psychism, or permits himself to take part in seances. The miseries caused by the ouija board, the fallacies of automatic writing, and the general hazard of psychic phenomena have ruined more than a few lives.

*QUESTION—How can a drone become useful at fifty? Now that I understand things better, I want to be useful.*

*Answer*—The first thing for you to do is to forget that you are fifty. Remember that you are an eternal self; that before the world existed, you were, and that after the world ends, you will still be. Time is an illusion, and greatness rises above time. Many of the greatest men and women of the world accomplish little, if anything, before fifty. When you think of accomplishment in philosophical terms, you are thinking of something that transcends time and place and becomes part of a cosmic plan of action, extending through hundreds of lives. Take stock of yourself. What have you learned in the fifty years of the present life? What do you know that others ought to know? What can you do that needs to be done? Remember that in the great craft of the Temple Builders, we all begin as apprentices. Our first task must always be something small and comparatively insignificant. The beginning of wisdom is to do the thing at hand. You may still need to spend time in the perfection of your own disposition, the mastery of temperament and attitude. You may still have responsibilities to others around you which have not been fulfilled. The example of what you have accomplished, and what philosophy has done for you, may be a great inspiration to those with whom you come in contact. Think noble thoughts, dream beautiful dreams, labor constructively from day to day, and when you are ready for a greater accomplishment, the work that you are to do will come to hand. The universe always has work for those who are qualified to perform it.

*QUESTION—Is a balance between introversion and extroversion best, even though introversion is associated with serious thought but no social contact?*

*Answer*—This is a psychological question involving factors little understood by even the most advanced psychologist. Introversion, or the subjectification of action, is a retiring from the circumference to the center of action. Except in rare cases, introversion results in inhibition, and inhibitions lead to most of the evils that afflict the metaphysically minded. On the other hand, extroversion—the complete objectification of self—is the phenomenon of energies rushing constantly from a center to the circumference. In introversion there is not enough expression, and in extroversion there is not enough control. It is the constant duty of the wise man to preserve a balance between expression and control.

Introversion is one of the most common diseases of the learned, and extroversion is the plague of the uninformed. Men who think much, do little; and with much action, there is usually small thought. To bind each action to an adequate reason, and to visualize each thought as manifesting in an appropriate consequence, is to keep open and well regulated the courses of energy in the human consciousness. A serious thinker must think seriously concerning the application of his thoughts to their reasonable ends in action. To think constantly and do nothing, is not the way to become wise. To weary the faculties with constant strain and never rest them through proper relaxation from mental effort, is to endanger the reason and impair the health. A well-balanced thinker always has a proper relaxation, and strives to prevent a narrowness of viewpoint by keeping in reasonably close contact at all times with other persons of different thoughts and ideas. Such a procedure will in the long run contribute more to the philosophy itself than constant application to abstractions.

*QUESTION—What place have insects in the scheme of evolution? Are they a legitimate life stream?*

*Answer*—In the old teachings, we learn that insect life is the survival of the earliest organisms that existed upon the earth. They are stragglers that were unable to keep up with the life waves to which they belonged. They have consequently gone through a certain retrogression, and will not be able to continue their unfoldment until the development of a new life wave. They might, therefore, be regarded as minute negative centers of life, exceedingly responsive to the mental impulses of higher organisms. The destructive tendencies in insect life are not really inherent to the insect, but are communicated to it by higher organisms. Thus insect pests, bacterial epidemics etc., are always aggravated by waves of destructiveness in human behavior. Insects are instruments of karma, and their viciousness is due to the viciousness in human thought and emotional impulses in the animal kingdom. There is an old tradition to the effect that when man achieves to the Golden Age, disease, sin and death will cease and the micro-organisms that now carry disease and torment men, will cease their activities. The story of the insect is concealed under the allegory of Pandora and her box.

*QUESTION—Do animals have consciousness after death? What is the difference between the spirit of an animal and that of man?*

*Answer*—Philosophy teaches that the Eternal Essence, which we call God, and which is the sum and origin of all things, is as much in the animal as it is in man, and therefore the plant of the field or the animal that roams among the hills is as surely an immortal creature as is man. The difference between the various forms of life that we see is not in the invisible spiritual nature within, but rather in the unfoldment of the objective vehicles by means of which the invisible nature manifests itself.

As the animal has not the rational faculties of man, man's sphere of consciousness after death would be inconceivable to creatures with plant or animal consciousness. But the law of evolution is gradually unfolding the potentialities of the lower kingdoms of nature, and in time, the animal will unfold its consciousness to a degree fully as great as that of man. All together, the mineral, the plant, the animal, and man are being swept along to endless stages of growth and unfoldment, until finally all attain to that perfection which is the ultimate condition of unity with Eternal Life.

Because the superphysical bodies of the animal are not highly individualized, there is little after-death consciousness. The animal soul or entity returns almost immediately to the physical world. The interval between incarnations is frequently only a few weeks, whereas man, who has a more highly individualized subjective nature, usually remains out of incarnation for at least one thousand years.

*QUESTION—If idealists believe in the sacredness of life, declaring it sinful to destroy even the smallest creatures, do they have any solution to the problem of what to do with vermin, bugs, and poisonous insects?*

*Answer*—In all matters of this kind, it is wise to realize that we are most truly philosophic when we accomplish the greatest good to the greatest number. Very often, by obeying the letter of the law, we crucify the spirit. The Jains, a very strict East Indian religious sect, employ a man to stand with a broom in front of their temples and tenderly whisk to one side all creeping and crawling things that may chance to stray across the pavement, so that no living thing will be injured or stepped on by passers-by. If, after the individual has used every precautionary measure, such as cleanliness etc., it becomes a matter where various pests are a menace to the community, it is then necessary to destroy them in order to accomplish the greatest good to the greatest number. For example, rats are very often carriers of plagues and epidemics that will sweep through whole districts and exact a terrific toll of human life.

It is quite impossible for an individual to live an absolutely harmless life. The very air he breathes contains minute organisms that must die in order that he may continue; the growing tree absorbs into itself the life of lesser plants and creatures, and thus lives at the expense of the weaker; the water we drink is a mass of animalicula that are just as surely alive as horses, dogs, and cattle. We may, and should, reduce our destructiveness to a minimum, but we cannot become entirely free of having to sacrifice other lives for our own survival. The point is this: if we must kill, it is also our duty to give life; if we must destroy, there is only one reason for our perpetuation—that we produce more than we destroy. If multitudes of lives must be sacrificed for our continuance, we owe to nature a debt that we can liquidate only by making the best possible use of the time given to us at so great a cost to other things.

The most foolish and wicked are those who do not realize what must die, that we may live. Therefore, if we must kill to live, let us not live to kill; but, using the energy that is given to us, dedicate our lives to constructive labors by which all humanity and nature may be benefited. In this way, we justify our existence. As the lesser is sacrificed for man, so man, in turn, must be willing to be sacrificed for something still greater in the cause of that Divine Power which is as far above man as man is above the reptiles and the vermin.

*QUESTION—Do people appreciate only what they pay well for? Please explain the money principle in connection with spiritual instruction.*

*Answer*—All neophytes entering the ancient Mystery Temples brought with them valuable gifts or such as they had; not because the gifts themselves were regarded as payment for instruction, but because only the individual who was willing to sacrifice the best that he had for that which he desired to know, was worthy of instruction. Money is a symbol of value in this modern world. The average person prizes it above every possession. Therefore, it is proper and suitable that he should give it as a symbol of sacrifice and appreciation for the priceless treasure he receives. Any person having much, and selfishly refusing to support adequately that which he believes, need not hope for any great measure of illumination. It is not the lack of the gift that will stand in his way, but the lack of the *spirit of giving.*

*QUESTION—If we are to do good, does it matter if we hurt people's feelings doing it?*

*Answer*—This question reminds me of an old friend, a Methodist minister, whose motto was, "If I don't hurt somebody's feelings, I'm not preaching the gospel." Seriously speaking, the whole answer to this question depends upon the interpretation of the word *good.* There are two kinds of illusionary good—my good and the other fellow's good. Both of these are often at direct variance with that Universal Good which alone is real. To do good is a fine art, and those who dabble in reform without a depth of wisdom, of vast tolerance, and great experience in life, often do more harm than good. It is true that we are to do good, but it is also true that we are to become wise, and it has been proved by experience that only those who are wise can really do good. When action is dominated by opinions, or selfishness, or sympathy, or any emotion or thought that is not grounded in actual fact, our efforts to do good usually lose the name of action.

It is well to bear in mind, in our efforts to do good, the Socratic definition of this virtue: "That which is true, necessary, and beautiful is good." Our most common mistake in attempting to do good is to overlook the factor of beauty in action. That is why we are likely to hurt people's feelings. Others often are not as offended by what is said as by the way it is said. There are beautiful ways to do everything, and they are usually acceptable; but when beauty fails in the deed, the deed itself misses its mark. Beauty is not weakness or sentiment; it is the divinity in the deed. Nowhere is beauty more needed in action than in reforms and corrections, and there is nowhere it is less likely to appear. It is true we are all here to do good, but if we do not wish our ministrations to inadvertently contribute to the world's evils, our labors must reflect the beauty and understanding that we have developed within ourselves.


*QUESTION—Please give an explanation of people being "divinely protected." We so often hear persons say that they have no fear of anything because they are divinely protected. Does not the law of cause and effect render this idea untenable?*

*Answer—*Most exponents of the cult of "divine protection" derive their ideas from one of several systems of mental metaphysics, which seek to make man right with his world by surrounding him with a wall of mental auto-suggestions. It would be folly to deny that mental attitude is capable of producing a marked effect upon the external life of the individual, but effects that are inconsistent with the spiritual facts of the individual's life are impermanent and consistently disastrous. All enlightened systems of philosophy and mysticism agree that it is impossible in the long run to fool the law of cause and effect. If by mental processes we attract to ourselves things that are not our own by merit, our very possessions become our misery and everything we gain is a loss to ourselves.

No person, under any condition, can be divinely protected from the effects he has set in motion by his own causations. He may build a mental wall of defense by which he temporarily deflects the thunderbolts of karma, but this is not divine protection—this is mortal will defying divinity. In the old fables, mortal will, under the name of Satan and his angels, defies the edict of heaven and sets up its kingdom in the abyss. Mental metaphysicians have much in common with the fallen angel. When we resist that which we have caused to come to us, when we refuse to acknowledge the debts we have made, when we surround ourselves with a wall of mental electricity, we are not divinely protected—we are simply resisting for a little while those consequences which must ultimately catch up with us. Worse than this, our attitude toward destiny being wrong, we usually are extravagant in our desires and unreasonable in our attitudes, thus bringing the sum of our debts much higher than it would normally be. The only protection with which we can safely surround ourselves is the invincible armor of our own integrity. Man is not protected by the gods, but by the honor that is within him.

*QUESTION—Please list the best works to read on the interpretation of the Grecian myths.*

*Answer—*The mythological writings of the Greeks are founded, for the most part, upon the secret tradition of the Orphics. According to the old records, Orpheus, whose name means "dark of skin" brought the ancient Wisdom Religion from India to the progenitors of the classical Hellenes. It is impossible to interpret Greek mythology philosophically without the Orphic keys. The writings of Homer and Hesiod were derived from the initiation pageantry of the Orphic cult, perpetuated in the Eleusinian and Dionysian Mysteries. Books dealing with this obscure subject in an enlightened manner are few, and for the most part rare. Of particular importance are the translations and writings of Thomas Taylor, the Platonist. His *Mystical Hymns of Orpheus* is important; also his *Dissertation on the Eleusinian and Bacchic Mysteries,* and his *Essay on the Odyssey of Homer* which serves as an appendix to his translations of the four books of Plotinus *On Abstinence From Animal Food.* Of more recent writers, probably the most reliable is G. R. S. Mead, whose splendid little work *Orpheus* is derived in some parts from original Greek sources. In other parts it is a summary of Thomas Taylor's researches.

*QUESTION—What is sorcery?*

*Answer—*Sorcery is black magic. In the ancient Atlantean world, a division took place in the occult arts. This resulted in what was called the two paths—white and black magic. White magicians were designated "masters of the right," and black magicians "masters of the left." The difference between white and black magic is essentially the difference in motive. White magic is founded upon unselfishness; black magic upon selfishness. A student of the ancient wisdom is white or black according to the merit of the impulse that urges him to accomplishment and action. Sorcery is the use of occult knowledge for selfish personal purposes at the expense of others. When we use superior wisdom to gain advantage over those more ignorant than we are, then we are sorcerers. When we use superior knowledge to aid and perfect others, then we are white magicians.

The natural magic used by medicine men and Shamans is not actual sorcery. It is part of the natural worship of aboriginal peoples who are able to control certain of the elements of nature so as to cause rain, thunder, lightning, and other natural phenomena. Natural magic, like the marvels of science, is impersonal; but the moment moral factors are involved, it becomes white or black according to its constructive or destructive use. Metaphysics today has in its ranks thousands of little parlor sorcerers—"thinking prosperity," meditating for power, and scheming occultly for superiority over each other.

*QUESTION—Is not a physical demonstration of prosperity an evidence that the person has accomplished an inner illumination and is able to control the law of supply and demand?*

*Answer*—This subject is larger than might first appear, involving several factors that must be considered separately. Persons possessing wealth must derive it from one of three sources: they either inherit it, acquire it through effort, or receive it through circumstances such as the accidents of gift or providence. In other words, they are born wealthy, achieve wealth, or have wealth thrust upon them. In any case, possession is an aspect of karma. If we believe philosophy, we must acknowledge that no one can possess a great measure of anything except by the decree of universal compensation. Anyone whose action causes wealth, will have wealth or its equivalent in this or a future life. However, this is only the beginning of the matter. Wealth is not an end, but an incident in the unfolding of human consciousness. Furthermore wealth is one of the heaviest burdens that a man must bear, for by its very nature it is a constant temptation to abuse and misuse.

Wealth is not as difficult to achieve as many people believe. Nearly anyone can become wealthy who is willing to sacrifice enough of other qualities to achieve wealth. It is a thousand times easier to be rich than it is to be wise, for shrewdness will accumulate money; but only an inner illumination, resulting from hundreds of lives devoted to truth and integrity, can result in perfect wisdom. I cannot see that wealth is any evidence of spiritual superiority. I would say, rather, that it is a great opportunity for the accomplishment of good. If this good is accomplished, it is termed in India a virtue, and out of the virtue of many lives, come wisdom and illumination. Soul power is not measured by possession, but by the enlightened use of possession. A life devoted to accumulation is not one to pattern after. Wealth, at best, is a material thing beset with material uncertainties and subject to all the vicissitudes of the physical state. He who possesses it is limited and narrowed by its responsibilities and worries.

If wealth descends upon an individual from his karma, it should be accepted with humility and resignation by the spiritually minded person. But to make wealth the goal of living, and to spend a lifetime in the accumulation of it, can scarcely be regarded as an enlightened course of action. Spirituality implies detachment, or more correctly, an attachment to real values. Each person highly prizes that which is the measure of his own consciousness. When unfolding reason reveals the beauty and desirability of spiritual things, the intellect inevitably turns from low values that no longer satisfy and are therefore no longer proper ends of effort. To say that the demonstration of material prosperity is an evidence of inner enlightenment, is to confuse two irreconcilable standards of value. We may as well say that wisdom is worth a dollar and a quarter, or that illumination is worth so much an hour. Spiritual values have no material equivalents, nor are they justified or manifested upon the physical plane. Render unto Caesar the things that are Caesar's, but do not try to confuse the law of the spirit with the ambitions of matter.

*QUESTION—Please explain the mystery of omens.*

*Answer*—Nearly all important events of history have been preceded by prophetic circumstances. Visions have appeared in the sky, like the mysterious sword of flame that hung over Jerusalem before its fall. Curious accidents have occurred presaging evil, and coming events have presented themselves as dreams and visions. Nearly all the great changes of human affairs have followed appropriate warning, and whole books have been written describing and proving the general occurrence of omens.

Occultism explains the appearance of strange portents of approaching fate in a very simple way. All major changes in the physical life of man, or his world, are the effects of causes that exist not in the physical world, but in the superphysical planes of the universe. An earthquake, for example, exists as an archetype or pattern in the invisible world long before the physical phenomenon takes place. Seismic cataclysms that will not occur in the material world for centuries already exist as archetypes in the superphysical body of the planet. These archetypes are established by the law of karma, and their force is built up by the repetition of the causes that originally precipitated the pattern.

Let us say, for example, that karma decrees that a continent and its inhabitants shall be submerged by volcanic forces. This fact, having been metaphysically established, is intensified by the destructive tendencies in the life and action of the doomed people. At last, after centuries of crystallization, the archetypal pattern reaches such definite proportions that this psychical pattern moves the physical elements into agreement with the metaphysical design or shape. It follows that archetypes in the process of crystallization become more and more tangible or physical. The result is that mediums, psychics, and other super-sensitive persons, may sense or see the archetype before the physical phenomenon is precipitated.

The increasing force building up in the archetype occasionally produces curious, unaccountable happenings. These happenings are not unlike the pranks played by electricity, under certain conditions, for the force behind all archetypes is basically electrical, but a far more subtle form of electricity than can be recognized by material science. Premonitions are truly coming events casting their shadows before them, because these events occur in the invisible world long before they can be felt in dense material forms. The archetypal ethers of the earth already carry locked within them the forms or patterns of all the important changes that will take place geologically or socially for the next several thousands of years.

The mind of man not only remembers the past, but plans the future, and the intellectual substances of the earth already bear the thought patterns of a wide variety of changes and achievements. All the inventions and as yet undiscovered secrets of nature, are plainly existent in the archetypal sphere, and it is from this world of patterns that men draw their discoveries, creations, and compositions. Mozart once observed that every piece of music that he composed he actually heard, as though played in the air by an invisible orchestra, before he wrote it down. Many great inventions have come as visions and dreams, for under certain circumstances, the creative type of mind can contact the sphere of archetypes where all things yet to be known exist as living pictures composed of vibrant ether.

*QUESTION—Is astrology a true science?*

*Answer*—Astrology and alchemy are the oldest sciences known to man. According to the traditions of the Hindus, the astrological arts were practiced by the Atlanteans, and descended from the peoples of the lost continent of Atlantis to the progenitors of the Aryans. Astrology has been cultivated by all civilized nations of the world. Richard Procter observed that no civilization has reached a high degree of culture without including astrology among its branches of learning.

It follows, then, that the effects of the heavenly bodies upon terrestrial affairs have been observed and recorded for many thousands of years. It would seem evident that no system of learning could have survived the vicissitudes of a hundred ages unless it was founded in demonstrable truth. The ancients convinced themselves by countless observations that the heavenly bodies not only influence mundane affairs, but that this influence is regular and consistent, and the elements thereof can be reduced to an exact science—the only exact prophetic science man has yet evolved.

Astrology should never be confused with astrologers, any more than laws should be confused with lawyers, medicine with doctors, and religion with theologians. Man, as an interpreter of universal truths, is limited in his interpretations by the inevitable imperfections in himself. In competent hands, astrology, at its present state of development, compares favorably with, shall we say, medicine, in the matter of accuracy. The physician cannot diagnose a disease infallibly, nor can the average astrologer predict infallibly. It would be entirely unreasonable to reject medicine because physicians make mistakes, and it is equally unreasonable to expect astrologers to be infallible when no other science is expected to exhibit infallibility either in its theories or its practice. Anyone working sincerely with astrology can easily convince himself that the science is founded upon sound and accurate principles. He can also prove that it works, and the occasional inconsistencies or exceptions that occur, only stimulate him to greater endeavor and more thorough acquaintance with the elements of his science.

There are too many accurate predictions recorded in history to deny prophecy. Too many people have had their character correctly analyzed, and the coming events of their lives correctly predicted, for astrology to be easily disproved. The mere fact that modern science denies astrology—without adequate examination—means nothing. The bodies of so-called learning are known to be extremely negative and critical in their attitude toward all occult and metaphysical matters. Science, however, has never disproved astrology, and never can. Maturity of thought will finally bring all forms of material learning back to the metaphysical foundations that were laid in the first ages of the world.

*QUESTION—Have we entered the Aquarian Age yet?*

*Answer*—There is some difficulty in determining astronomically the actual time of the sun's ingress into a zodiacal sign. Certain arbitrary factors must be accepted before any satisfactory calculation is possible. According to the opinions of modern astronomers, the sun is now in about the 8th degree of Pisces, and has therefore about 8 degrees yet to retire before it retrogrades by the precessional motion out of the sign and into Aquarius. The precessional motion is about 1 degree in 72 years. According to this calculation, it will be nearly 600 years before the sun actually enters the sign of Aquarius, at the equinox, and the Aquarian Age has its beginning. Of course, the sun changes degree every 72 years, and these degree changes are in themselves capable of producing a considerable change in the life of man. I know that several metaphysical movements are of the opinion that we have already entered the Aquarian Age, or will very soon do so, but I do not believe that these organizations can justify their opinions astronomically.

*QUESTION—Has the Sixth Root Race started to appear upon the earth?*

*Answer*—According to the metaphysical philosophy of the Brahmans, human life upon the earth manifests through seven out-pourings, which are called *races*. The first of these races is called the Polarian, and inhabited a vast polar continent hundreds of millions of years ago. The second was the Hyperborean, referred to by the Greeks as a semi-divine race dwelling in the land north of the winds. The third was the Lemurian, a dark civilization existing upon a continent involving what is now the Indian Ocean and the Australian Archipelago. The fourth was the Atlantean, whose great island-continent filled a considerable part of what is now called the Atlantic Ocean, extending from Greenland on the north, to a southern latitude approximately parallel with Brazil. The fifth, to which we now belong, is called the Aryan, and had its origin in North Central Asia about a million years ago. The sixth and seventh races are yet to come. The sixth race will be derived from the highest types produced by the fifth race, and may spring up among several progressive peoples simultaneously.

The application of the term "sixth root race" personality, to describe a precocious or unusual type of human being, is a figure of speech rather than a scientific fact. I question very much if true sixth-root-race types are as yet appearing, as many thousands of years must pass before the advent of the sixth race. It is quite possible, however, that tendencies that will later develop into sixth-root-race qualities are beginning to appear as progressive impulses in our present society. Some believe that the sixth root race will emerge from the chemistry of inter-racial mingling in America. Others feel that Russia is the logical cradle, inasmuch as great social experiments are being carried on there. Australia has also been advanced as a possible field for sixth-root-race activities. It is my opinion that pioneers from several subdivisions of our present race will form the nucleus for the future human type, and that when the time comes for the sixth race to be objectified from the physical world, a new continent will rise, probably in the Pacific Ocean, to serve as a theater of action for the new race.

*QUESTION—Do you believe that we are about to enter the Golden Age?*

*Answer—*In the mythology of the Greeks, the life of the earth is divided into four great periods, called Ages. The first was the Golden Age, the second the Age of Silver, the third the Bronze Age, and the fourth the Age of Iron. These Ages correspond with the Yugas of the Hindus, which also divide the cycles of evolution into quaternary periods. The Golden Age of the Greeks is described by the poets as a time in which no evil existed, and all nature dwelt together in beauty and harmony. Neither sin nor death had come into the world, and Pandora's box, with all its ills, had never been opened to loose its misfortunes upon man. For thousands of years, the idealists of the race have dreamed of the return of the Golden Age. They have envisioned man growing wiser and less selfish, evil ceasing and humanity restored at last to an enlightened and cooperative condition.

There is no evidence, however, at the present time, that we are in any imminent danger of a general reform. Men grow more selfish with each passing day, and we must experience much more of sorrow and suffering before we will voluntarily dedicate ourselves to a program of enlightenment. We now live in the Age of Iron, or the Kali-yuga or Black Age of the Hindus. Until this cycle ends—and alas many thousands of years remain yet to run—we cannot look for the return of the paradisiacal state described in the ancient fables. Yet the Golden Age must finally come again, for all the progress of the race—though slow and apparently uncertain—is leading inevitably to a better day when humanity, tired of self-inflicted woes, will depart from its present course of evil and bring to reality the utopias of its dreams.

*QUESTION—What is the most useful thing in this world?*

*Answer*—Many people will differ in answering this question. Some might say electricity, others printing, others the telephone. Probably no better answer to this question can be found than that which Thales gave to the Pharaoh of Egypt. The great Greek sophist said: "Virtue is the most useful thing in the world, for by the presence of it all other things are made beautiful and good, and without it even the most spectacular accomplishment is hurtful and incomplete."